SECURITY AND DEFENCE IN THE TERRORIST ERA

FOREIGN POLICY, SECURITY AND STRATEGIC STUDIES

Editors: Alex Macleod and Charles-Philippe David

The Foreign Policy, Security and Strategic Studies Series seeks to promote analysis of the transformation and adaptation of foreign and security policies in the post Cold War era. The series welcomes manuscripts offering innovative interpretations or new theoretical approaches to these questions, whether dealing with specific strategic or policy issues or with the evolving concept of security itself.

Security and Defence in the Terrorist Era

Canada and North America

ELINOR C. SLOAN

The Centre for Security and Foreign Policy Studies
and
The Raoul-Dandurand Chair of Strategic and Diplomatic Studies

McGill-Queen's University Press
Montreal & Kingston · London · Ithaca

© McGill-Queen's University Press 2005
ISBN 0-7735-2973-X

Legal deposit fourth quarter 2005
Bibliothèque nationale du Québec

Printed in Canada on acid-free paper that is 100%
ancient forest free (100% post-consumer recycled),
processed chlorine free.

This book has been published with the help
of a grant from the Canadian Federation for the
Humanities and Social Sciences, through the Aid
to Scholarly Publications Programme, using funds
provided by the Social Sciences and Humanities
Research Council of Canada.

McGill-Queen's University Press acknowledges the
support of the Canada Council for the Arts for our
publishing program. We also acknowledge the
financial support of the Government of Canada
through the Book Publishing Industry Development
Program (BPIDP) for our publishing activities.

Library and Archives Canada Cataloguing in Publication

Sloan, Elinor C. (Elinor Camille), 1965-
     Security and defence in the terrorist era : Canada
and North America / Elinor C. Sloan.

Includes bibliographical references and index.
ISBN 0-7735-2973-X

1. National security--Canada. 2. Canada--Defenses.
3. United States--Defenses. I. Title.

UA22.S57 2005   355'.033071   C2005-903741-5
F1030.7.B63 2000

Typeset in Palatino 10.5/13
by Infoscan Collette, Quebec City

For my students

Contents

SECURITY AND DEFENCE IN THE TERRORIST ERA

Introduction

No responsibility is more fundamental to a federal government than providing for the security of citizens. Since World War II, modern, democratic governments have progressively taken on a multitude of responsibilities with respect to their country's citizens, each meant in some way to better their daily lives. But, in the final analysis, these pale in comparison to the original and most fundamental element of the social contract between the individual and the state: that people give up a certain measure of freedom in return for government-provided security.

"Security," here, is the absence of threat to a particular set of values. What this set of values includes differs among countries and could even differ between successive governments of one country. Nonetheless, it can be argued that Canadians adhere to a commonly agreed-upon set of values that must be guaranteed. National security, Canada's National Defence College argues, "includes freedom from military attack or coercion, freedom from internal subversion and freedom from the erosion of the political, economic and social values which are essential to our quality of life."[1] Freedom from military attack and internal subversion, in turn, can be elaborated to include the physical security of our national territory, our territorial integrity, the safety of our nation's citizens, and the protection of our critical infrastructures. Those political, economic, and social values that are essential to the quality of our lives include national sovereignty, democracy and the rule of law, individual rights and freedoms, and a certain measure of economic well-being.

In principle, there could be any number of threats to national security; that is, threats to those values I have listed. To provide the analytic boundaries necessary for any meaningful policy prescription we must ascribe some sort of time frame to the concept of threat. In this context, a threat to national security can be seen as an action or sequence of events that threatens drastically and over a relatively brief span of time to degrade one or more of the values Canadians deem essential to their way of life.[2] A national security strategy involves measures designed to guard against these threats. Both military and non-military instruments will be involved. Defence policy is a derivative of security policy in that it is meant to address the specific range of threats against which military force is perceived to be a necessary or primary instrument of action.[3] In theory, security policy serves as a bridge between defence policy and a country's broader foreign policy.[4]

Throughout most of its history, Canada's national security strategy has been implicit in the actions and policies of the government of the day rather than explicitly stated.[5] Moreover, with the possible exceptions of the Trudeau government in the early 1970s and the minority government of Paul Martin, Canadian governments have always placed primary emphasis on looking overseas to address potential threats to the country. The structure of Canada's fireproof house began to weaken early in the past century with the invention of the airplane and subsequently the advent of intercontinental flight. It became even more unsteady by mid-century with the development and deployment of intercontinental ballistic missiles. But the fact that there was never a superpower standoff during the Cold War meant that the house was not truly destroyed until 11 September 2001.

Today it makes no sense to talk individually about Canadian security, North American security, and international peace and security; all three are closely intertwined. Our national security is inextricably related to that of our southern neighbour and to events and circumstances around the world. The imperative in a world of growing and unprecedented interdependence, where developments on the other side of the globe can impact us next door, is to examine and integrate into a whole the homeland security, homeland defence, and overseas military and civilian requirements for Canadian security and defence.

How can the Canadian government best provide for the security of Canadians in the post-9/11 era? What balance should it find between "offensive" measures abroad and "defensive" measures at home in guaranteeing the security of its citizens? These are the questions that this book seeks to answer. Canadian security and defence requirements of the future can be roughly divided into four categories: military responses at home (homeland defence); civilian responses at home (homeland security); military responses abroad (warfighting and stabilization operations); and civilian responses abroad (for example, development aid and diplomacy). This book centres on the first three quadrants of responses and where the Canadian government could best place its emphasis. The fourth quadrant, civilian responses abroad, falls squarely in the realm of foreign policy and will be addressed only insofar as it pertains directly to Canadian security.

Chapter 1 sets out a proposed conceptual framework for determining the relative emphasis to be placed on offensive or defensive measures in Canada's national security strategy, a modified version of offence-defence theory, while chapter 2 examines the nature of the threat to North America, a key element in the calculation. Chapter 3 highlights the evolution of US thinking about threats to the North American continent during the first post–Cold War decade, thereby providing the context for post-9/11 developments. Chapter 4 provides an overview and analysis of the numerous homeland security initiatives that have been taken jointly or separately by the United States and Canada since the 9/11 attacks, while chapter 5 focuses on homeland defence issues. Both examine areas of ongoing contention or debate and put forward some proposed solutions. Chapter 6 addresses a specific aspect of the homeland defence debate – space and ballistic missile defence – while chapter 7 takes the analysis to the offensive dimension, examining the military requirements for addressing threats to North America overseas, before they reach our shores. It also looks at Canadian military capabilities in these areas. The final chapter gives guidance as to what balance Canada should find in providing for its security offensively abroad or defensively at home, and it concludes with a window on the broader civilian and diplomatic measures that are necessary if the Canadian government is to guarantee the security of its citizens.

1

Offence and Defence in the Terrorist Era

One method of ascertaining the relative emphasis to be placed on offensive or defensive strategies in Canada's national security strategy may be through the conceptual framework of a modified version of offence-defence theory. This theory argues that there is an offence-defence balance that determines the relative efficacy of offensive and defensive security strategies.[1] The theory is premised on the notion that it is possible to determine where the balance falls between the dominance of the offence and the dominance of the defence. To say the offence has the advantage means that "it is easier to destroy the other's army and take its territory than it is to defend one's own"; to say the defence has the advantage means that "it is easier to protect and to hold than it is to move forward, destroy and take."[2] Where the pendulum falls between these two extremes determines the offence-defence balance and whether a state would be best to choose an offensive or a defensive security strategy.

Elements of offence-defence theory can be traced to early Cold War writings and even further back to arms control conferences in the interwar period.[3] Nonetheless, the theory itself did not come to prominence until the late 1970s, with the publication of a groundbreaking article on the security dilemma by Robert Jervis.[4] Since that time, the theory has been used to explain a wide range of international phenomena, including alliance behaviour, nuclear strategy and policy, and conventional arms control, among others.[5] Offence-defence theory is notable for the light it sheds on the incidence or non-incidence of war: the theory holds that international conflict is more likely when the offence has the advantage, and that peace and cooperation are more likely when defence has the advantage.[6]

Numerous criticisms of offence-defence theory have emerged in the scholarly literature. The case is made that the theory is inoperative because it is difficult to classify a weapon as offensive or defensive; because states rarely perceive the offence-defence balance correctly; because other variables are more important causes of war, peace, and security policy; because the balance always favours the defence and therefore can explain little, as it does not vary;[7] and because, in any case, the offence-defence balance cannot be measured, since the outcomes of wars are so uncertain.[8] These criticisms have been refuted by further scholarly work arguing that in fact offence-defence theory does not depend on whether offensive and defensive weapons can be distinguished;[9] that shifts in the offence-defence balance do take place and have a great effect on the risk of war;[10] and that there are strong grounds for concluding that states can measure the offence-defence balance.[11]

OFFENCE-DEFENCE THEORY: A POST-9/11 CRITIQUE

Offence-defence theory as currently formulated has two important shortfalls. First, its most common usage, a calculation involving two states, is not relevant to many of the issues policy-makers must face in the post-9/11 security environment. Second, in the past the theory has centred primarily (though not exclusively) on policy explanation and has not placed sufficient emphasis on policy prescription. It follows that the objective of this chapter is twofold: to make offence-defence theory, and specifically the manner in which the offence-defence balance is calculated, more relevant in the post-9/11 era; and to thereby enable the theory to be a better guide for decision makers in developing a national security strategy.

Offence-defence theory as it is most commonly used does not adequately inform us about the post-9/11 world. This is primarily because of the actor units on which the theory focuses. The offence-defence balance has been succinctly defined as "the ratio of the cost of offensive forces to the cost of defensive capabilities."[12] Implicit in most elaborations of this definition is that we are speaking of offensive capabilities on the part of state A and defensive capabilities on the part of state B. Robert Jervis, for example, defines the balance in the following terms: "Does the state have to spend more or less than one dollar on defensive forces to offset each dollar spent by the other side on forces that could be used to attack?"[13] Charles Glaser and Chaim Kaufmann explain the offence-defence balance as "the ratio of the cost of the forces that the attacker requires to take territory to the cost of the defender's forces."[14] Sean Lynn-Jones frames the balance in terms of "the amount of resources that a state must invest in offense (or defense) to offset an adversary's investment in defense (or offense)."[15] And Robert Gilpin argues that "To speak of a shift in favor of the offense [by state A] means that fewer resources than before must be expended on the offense in order to overcome the defense [by state B]."[16]

This framework is of limited usefulness in determining an appropriate response to the contemporary environment. Offence-defence theory is premised on a balance that is calculated by looking at the circumstances of two states – state A and state B – whereas the primary threat to the Western world today is the essentially stateless one of international terrorism. In many current situations, state A is not facing state B but rather a non-state actor. Moreover, the offence-defence balance is said to depend on how much territory the attacker is trying to take,[17] and yet "taking territory" is not a central objective of international terrorists. The real question today is whether it is easier or more effective for a state to seek security for itself against a non-state actor through the use of defensive measures at home or offensive measures abroad. As Glaser and Kaufmann so accurately point out, "the most common usage of the concept of the offense-defense balance does not determine whether security-seeking states should prefer offense or defense."[18]

A second reason offence-defence theory does not adequately inform us about the post-9/11 security environment is that the weight attached to one of the factors that has traditionally been considered as influencing the balance – geography – has not been reassessed to reflect contemporary realities. According to offence-defence theory, anything that impedes the attacker's ability to access or cross the defender's territory – whether it be mountain ranges, deserts, oceans, or large rivers – favours the defence.[19]

The exposed plains of Eastern Europe, for example, are often cited as being more favourable to conquest than the more mountainous areas of Western Europe. Similarly, the United States and Great Britain have historically been said to have defensible geography by virtue of the fact that they are surrounded by large bodies of water.[20]

But the hindering role of geography is becoming less apparent. On 11 September 2001, international terrorism was able reach across oceans into downtown America. The increased dependence of Western societies on information technology has given rise to information warfare, which knows no borders in an increasingly interconnected world. And every day dozens of ships enter North American ports bearing thousands of containers, some of which, we fear, may hold weapons of mass destruction. The declining importance of geography points to the need to include the nature of the threat in the range of factors that impact the outcome of the offence-defence calculation. Thus, a third reason offence-defence theory as currently formulated does not provide policy-makers with adequate guidance is that the factors that have traditionally been considered to influence the offence and defence do not incorporate the range of issues now necessary for a more realistic assessment of the balance.

OFFENCE AND DEFENCE
IN THE TERRORIST ERA

To make offence-defence theory more relevant to the post-9/11 era, we need to modify the theory so that it focuses on the offensive and defensive capabilities of a single state. It must incorporate a state A/state A calculation of that state's defensive and offensive capabilities against a faceless enemy, as opposed to a state A/state B calculation focused on the offensive forces of one state and the defensive capabilities of another. In this modified version, offence dominance means that given the factors of technology, geography, and the nature of the threat, it is relatively easier to address threats to state A at their source abroad. Defence dominance means that given the same factors, it is relatively easier to defend against these threats at home. Defence, in turn, can be usefully elaborated to mean "techniques and actions, both active and passive, to repel attack, to protect people and property, to hold territory, and to minimize damage by the attacker."[21] This definition has significant resonance with today's homeland security and defence initiatives. Within the new framework, the offence-defence balance is redefined as follows: "If a state has one dollar to spend on national security, is it more cost-effective in security terms for it to spend that dollar on defensive measures and forces at home or on offensive forces for operations abroad?" In both cases the objective is to reduce the threat to, or increase the security of, the territory of the state in question. The answer will be relative, not absolute, since a certain degree of emphasis on both offensive and defensive measures will inevitably be required.

Beyond this, four additional modifications are required to make the theory more relevant to the contemporary security environment. First, the range of factors used to calculate the offence-defence balance needs to be expanded. Technology and geography have traditionally been seen as the two main factors that determine whether the offence or defence has the advantage. More recent scholarly work has broadened this list to include the size of forces, the cumulativeness of resources, nationalism, the domestic social and political order, and diplomatic factors such as the existence of collective security systems and defensive alliances.[22] The nature of the threat should be added to this list. Indeed, in the post-9/11 security environment the starting point in determining the offence-defence balance must be a close examination of the character of the threat the Western world is facing. The questions that might be addressed in this area include: What are the primary threats to North America today? What are the motivating factors for these threats? How easy/difficult is it to detect these threats? What would be the contemporary equivalent of the former strategy of looking for armies massing?

Second, one of the traditional factors used to calculate the offence-defence balance – geography – needs to be updated to reflect contemporary circumstances. In the past, analysis in this area centred on the fact that barriers to movement and distance generally favoured defenders,[23] and that national borders coinciding with natural barriers that impede offensive movement hindered conquest.[24] By contrast, future trade-off calculations must incorporate the impact of globalization on previously held geographic advantages and consider the ease with which adversaries, by virtue of the onward march of technology, can now overcome the geographical constraints of yesterday. Questions that might be addressed in this area include: What is the general geographic situation of the state concerned? How have global economic trends, new technologies, and attributes of the threat impacted previously held geographic advantages?

Third, the analysis must incorporate advances in civilian technologies. Civilian technologies have played an important role in military affairs for centuries. A good example is the railroad – its introduction transformed the ability of militaries to move large forces over great distances. But what is notable in the information age, which first took hold in the 1970s, is that civilian technologies have become ever more central, both to the conduct of military operations abroad and to a state's ability to combat threats at home. Commercial satellites, to give only one example, are used extensively for everything from providing military communications abroad, to pinpointing precision weapons coordinates, to monitoring North American airspace. Questions that need to be addressed in this area include: What advances have been made in civilian technologies for detecting/addressing contemporary threats to North America? Can they tackle the enormous task of monitoring transborder activity by sea, land, and air?

Finally, the other factor traditionally used to calculate the balance – military technology – continues to be relevant and should be examined as a means of addressing the threat. "Military technology" refers to the nature of the military weapons themselves and whether these weapons are best suited to defending territory or conducting offensive operations. The scholarly work reflects substantial debate over whether a military technology can be classified as offensive or defensive.[25] The discussion centres on the fact that many technologies, from tanks to strike aircraft and even military fortifications, can arguably be said to support both the offence and the defence. Nonetheless, there are certain technologies that are of relatively greater utility in either an offensive or defensive capacity. Fortifications are the most obvious example of a primarily defensive military technology. Mobility and striking power (the impact of the blow) have been identified as the essential characteristics of an offensive weapon.[26] More specifically, six major areas of technology are considered relevant to the offence and, by extension, to addressing threats abroad: mobility, firepower, protection, logistics, communications, and detection.[27]

Questions that need to be addressed in the area of military technology include: What is the character of contemporary advances in military technology? How applicable are they to deterring threats, striking terrorist organizations abroad, and defending the homeland?

Modifying offence-defence theory in this manner would transform the theory from one that primarily provides an explanation of international phenomena to one that is policy prescriptive. The main goal of offence-defence theory in the past has been to explain the behaviour of states based on the material constraints of the international system.[28] A modified version of offence-defence theory as presented here would have as its objective not an explanation of behaviour after the fact, but a proposal for future action. Modified offence-defence theory would provide US and Canadian policy-makers with guidance on whether relative budgetary emphasis should be placed on homeland security and defence measures in North America or on activities to address terrorism overseas, including the use of military force, diplomacy, and/or foreign aid.

CONCLUSION

In international politics, one scholar argues, states have two basic strategic options for maximizing their security: defensive and offensive.[29] They can adopt a defensive strategy to defend their territory, or they can adopt an offensive strategy to quell threats abroad. The challenge today is to make this conceptual framework relevant to the post-9/11 security environment. The offence-defence balance has traditionally been defined as the amount of resources a state must invest in offence to offset an adversary's investment in defence. But in an era when the adversary is often a faceless non-state actor, state A/state B calculations will in many cases be irrelevant. In these situations, offence or defence dominance will be influenced in part by advances in military and civilian technologies, and also in part by geography, although to a lesser degree than in previous historical periods. More than ever, a key factor to consider when choosing a preponderantly offensive or defensive strategy will be the nature of the threat.

2

The Nature of the Threat

The starting point for determining the relative emphasis to be placed on defensive strategies at home and offensive strategies abroad for guaranteeing Canadian security is an appreciation of the nature of the threat to North America. This chapter begins with an overall look at the threat to the United States and Canada and then examines in more detail the changing strategic options, motives, and capabilities that make up this threat assessment. It concludes that policy changes cannot eliminate the threat in the short-to-medium term, and that ultimately Canadian security will depend upon finding and implementing the right combination of offensive and defensive military and civilian measures.

THE THREAT TO AMERICA

International Terrorism

In testimony before Congress six months after the terrorist attacks on New York and Washington, former director of central intelligence (DCI) and director of the Central Intelligence Agency (CIA) George Tenet stated that the most immediate and serious threat to the United States was international terrorism.[1] Terrorism can be defined as "the use of violence by nonstate entities against the institutions or citizens of states for political or ideological purposes, in a manner calculated to produce maximum shock and fear effect because of its apparently random and senseless character."[2] Its central elements include the creation of fear, the seemingly random use of violence, and attacks on the innocent.[3] Tenet focused his remarks on the threat Osama Bin Laden and the Al Qaeda network continued to pose to the United States and its interests abroad, notwithstanding the progress that had been made in Afghanistan in disrupting the network.

A year later Tenet had some successes to report in America's battle against Al Qaeda. More than a third of the top Al Qaeda leadership identified before the war had been killed or captured, and some 3,000 suspected Al Qaeda members had been detained in more than one hundred countries.[4] The US Department of State corroborated that thousands of Al Qaeda members had been detained and more than one-third of Al Qaeda's top leadership had been killed or captured, including some who conspired in the 11 September 2001 attacks, the attack on the uss *Cole* in 2000, and the bombings of two US embassies in East Africa in 1998.[5] By the second anniversary of 9/11, this figure had risen to about two-thirds of the Al Qaeda leadership.[6]

Removing top leadership figures is seen by US intelligence as especially important in combating terrorism. Although thousands of people have been trained at Al Qaeda camps, only the senior leadership is thought to have the connections and financing necessary to prosecute a major attack. "The loss of so many senior operational coordinators," argues one US intelligence report, "represents the elimination of a decade worth of terrorism planning experience. These individuals were, in large part, the guiding force behind the success of Al Qaeda's attacks."[7] Nonetheless, the CIA stresses that the Al Qaeda network is still dedicated to striking the US homeland and continues to pose a clear threat to the United States. "The network is extensive and adaptable ... Al Qaeda will try to adapt to changing circumstances as it regroups. It will seek a more secure base area so that it can pause from flight and resume planning. The bottom line ... is that Al Qaeda is living in the expectation of resuming the offensive."[8] Al Qaeda, in short, remains as committed as ever to attacking the US homeland.[9]

Both the CIA and MI5, the British security service, say that there is little prospect of a significant reduction in the threat of Islamic terrorism before the end of this decade.[10] Experts point out that the pattern of global terrorism grew more intense in the second year following the 11 September attacks, with bombings in Bali, Casablanca, Jakarta, Karachi, Mombasa, Riyadh, and Tunisia.[11] Capable replacements for leaders who have been killed appear to be emerging, some of whom have already proven their ability to carry out previously planned operations.[12] With their Afghanistan refuge severely disrupted, these new leaders are thought to be based in Saudi Arabia, in Iran, along the Pakistan-Afghanistan border, and in Indonesia.[13] It is unlikely, then, that the death or capture of Osama Bin Laden would bring an end to terrorist activity against the United States and its allies.[14] Even if the entire Al Qaeda leadership were eradicated, there is no guarantee that it would eliminate the threat. The CIA assesses that the steady spread of Al Qaeda's anti-US sentiment through the wider Sunni extremist movement ensures that a serious threat will remain for the foreseeable future – with or without Al Qaeda in the picture.[15]

According to both the Federal Bureau of Investigation (FBI) and the CIA, a number of terrorist attacks have been planned and thwarted against high-profile government or private facilities, famous landmarks, and US infrastructure nodes such as airports, bridges, harbours, and dams.[16] High-profile events such the Olympics and the Super Bowl, along with national elections, also attract terrorists intent on making another strike in the United States that would command worldwide attention. The *Global Terrorism Index*, produced by the London-based World Markets Research Centre, argues that a large-scale terrorist attack in the United States is "highly likely" as a result of that country's continuing battle with Al Qaeda and its large number of internationally known landmarks.[17] The CIA has stressed that although all of the attacks since 9/11 have occurred abroad, this does not in any way mean that the threat to the US homeland has waned.[18]

Although the 11 September attacks suggest that Al Qaeda and other terrorists will continue to use conventional weapons, one of the CIA's biggest concerns is that the "next" terrorist attack on American soil could involve weapons of mass destruction (WMD) – that is, chemical, biological, radiological, or even nuclear weapons. This prospect has been raised repeatedly as a grave concern by US intelligence, and outside experts have sounded the bell even louder. Harvard's Richard Falkenrath, for example, argued some years ago that "future acts of NBC [nuclear, biological, chemical] terrorism should be regarded as likely enough to place this threat among the most serious national security challenges faced by modern liberal democracies … [the likelihood of such acts] is low, but it is not zero, and it is rising."[19] Similarly, soon after 9/11

former secretary of defence William Perry stated, "Nuclear or biological weapons in the hands of terrorists constitute the single
greatest danger to American security, and a threat that is becoming increasingly less remote."[20]

Closely linked to growing concern about weapons of mass
destruction is a marked change in the nature of terrorism over the
past decade. "Old terrorism," noted the *Economist* in a survey
published soon after the 1998 terrorist bombings of American
embassies in Africa, generally had a specific political objective,
such as the overthrow of a colonial power. Perpetrators of the "old
terrorism" were careful to keep casualties to a minimum so as to
maintain their group's political legitimacy and increase its chances
of achieving its goal.[21] Limited political aims, a strategy of controlled
violence for achieving them, and an interest in self-preservation
were the hallmarks of terrorist activity throughout the post–World
War II period.[22]

But by the mid-1990s it was clear that the "old terrorism" had
begun to break down. New groups had emerged with vague
objectives, using violence for its own sake rather than to advance
an explicit political agenda, demonstrating no overriding concern
for self-preservation, and, most ominously, seeking to produce an
ever greater number of casualties. The increase in the number of
casualties per incident, combined with the sarin gas attack in
Tokyo in 1995, gave rise to the view that terrorists could seek mass
casualties through the use of weapons of mass destruction. "Long
before 11 September," one terrorism expert has pointed out, "there
was concern that international terrorism might be entering a new,
more dangerous phase."[23]

The CIA is also alert to the possibility of a cyber-warfare attack
by terrorists. The increasing dependence of Western societies on
computer systems and networks has created vulnerabilities that
can be exploited. Critical infrastructures at risk of a cyber-war
attack include those of transportation, oil and gas production and
storage, water supply, emergency services, banking and finance,
electrical power, and information and communications. US intelligence has argued that such attacks will become an increasingly
viable option for terrorists as they and other foreign adversaries
become more familiar with these targets and the technologies that
are required to attack them. Evidence suggests that Al Qaeda has
spent considerably more time mapping US vulnerabilities in
cyberspace than was previously thought by US analysts.[24]

Rogue States

In testimony before Congress, former DCI Tenet went beyond discussing the terrorist threat to mention the threat that so-called rogue states, also referred to as "states of concern," pose to the United States. The "rogue state" is defined by the September 2002 *National Security Strategy of the United States* as one that brutalizes its own people and squanders its national resources for the personal gain of its rulers; threatens its neighbours and violates international treaties to which it is party; attempts to acquire weapons of mass destruction to achieve its aggressive designs; sponsors terrorism around the globe; and rejects basic human values.[25]

Rogue states may pose an indirect threat to the United States by supporting terrorism. Although state sponsors assume a lower profile today than they did a decade ago, they remain a cause for concern. The State Department has found that although Libya and Sudan have taken significant steps towards cooperating in the global war on terrorism, the other designated state sponsors of terrorism – Cuba, Iran, North Korea, and Syria – have not taken all the actions necessary to sever their ties to terrorism.[26] That said, scholars have traced a gradual transition at the end of the twentieth century away from direct state sponsorship of terrorism and towards more amorphous groups, often having access to state resources but less and less likely to be under state control.[27] This is a potentially serious development, considering that unlike rogue states, international terrorists are not in control of territory that can be threatened or targeted with a view to bringing about a change in behaviour. The transnational, globally networked, and "protean" nature of the terrorist threat, [28] like that posed by Al Qaeda, makes the international terrorist an especially difficult foe to defeat.

Finally, US intelligence draws attention to the possibility that certain rogue states present a direct threat to North America. In this regard the country of greatest concern to the United States is North Korea, which has a declared nuclear weapons capability and is in the process of developing ballistic missiles with sufficient range to reach targets throughout North America. In addition to the long-standing threats from Russian and Chinese missile forces, the CIA argues, the United States faces a near-term intercontinental ballistic missile threat from North Korea, and over the next several years it could face a similar threat from Iran.[29]

THE THREAT TO CANADA

Reports by the Canadian Security Intelligence Service (CSIS) also indicate that the primary threat to the physical security and safety of Canadian citizens, as well as to the country's critical infrastructures, is international terrorism. In its first public report following 9/11, CSIS determined that Canada is at risk of being targeted directly or indirectly by Sunni Islamic terrorists.[30] High-ranking officials in the Department of National Defence have echoed that the most serious, direct threat faced by Canada is terrorism.[31]

Although Canada does not have the exposure of the United States, Canadians nonetheless have a number of things to fear from terrorism. Canada's proximity to the United States, its close ties to that country, the openness of its society to the movement of people and money, and its multiethnic population make it attractive to terrorists as a safe haven. "There are more international terrorist organizations currently active in Canada than anywhere else in the world," argues a RAND report on the issue, "with the possible exception of the United States."[32] In addition, because of the close ties between the two countries, there are a number of American assets in Canada that could be targeted for attack. Moreover, Canada's friendship for, and support of, the United States – including its participation in the war in Afghanistan in 2001 and 2002 – could result in Canada or Canadians being targeted for attack.[33] For all these reasons, "Canadians should not feel we are insulated from terrorism."[34] Although Canada may not be "the bull's eye in the sights of most extremists," it is "clearly positioned as one of the inner rings on the target."[35]

The CSIS 2002 *Public Report* also highlighted changes in the nature of terrorist activity in Canada. Specifically, it noted that Canada was no longer used by terrorist organizations strictly for logistical or support activities and had become a staging ground for terrorist acts. The well-known and often cited case is that of Ahmed Ressam, a member of a Montreal-based terrorist cell arrested late in 1999 while trying to enter the United States for the purposes of carrying out a terrorist attack. Up until then it was believed that Muslim radicals saw Canada mainly as a safe outpost from which they could engage in fundraising, recruitment, and other activities to support terrorist networks abroad.

Proximity of Canada to the United States is an important dimension of the threat to Canada. The *Global Terrorism Index* rated

Canada as the seventy-ninth most likely country to be attacked out of 186 countries surveyed. But this survey did not examine the use of countries as staging grounds for attacks elsewhere in the world, and especially in the United States, which is one of Canada's major terrorist problems. Apart from the possibility of transborder terrorist activity, as was averted in the Ressam case, officials at the US Department of Homeland Security are concerned about terrorists targeting flights that take off and land in Canada but come close enough to US soil to be used to launch an attack.[36] In addition, homeland security experts have stressed the need to think in terms of threats to shared critical infrastructure rather than transborder activity. Most of the northeastern United States, for example, is powered by hydroelectric plants in Quebec and would therefore make an attractive terrorist target.[37]

More recent csis public reports have revealed a heightened threat assessment. Taking into account the November 2002 statement by Osama Bin Laden naming six Western countries, including Canada, as targets of retribution because of their military support of the war on terrorism in Afghanistan,[38] csis has acknowledged that "Canada is directly threatened by terrorism."[39] Similarly, Canada's first national security adviser has stated that it is "absurd" to believe that terrorists will not attack Canada, noting that most of the six Western countries named by Bin Laden have already been attacked.[40] He continues to stress that there are real threats to Canada.[41] Like US intelligence agencies, csis is particularly concerned about the potential terrorist use of weapons of mass destruction. The security service also draws our attention to the threat of information warfare, stating that Canada's dependence on computer networks for the smooth functioning of its critical infrastructures has made the protection of these networks increasingly a matter of national security.[42]

csis has also prompted a new focus on rogue states. Countries such as Iran, Syria, and Libya, the security service points out, continue to provide terrorist organizations with training, arms, money, materials, and logistical support. csis notes that many of the countries that are attempting to develop wmd also continue to support terrorism as an instrument of national policy. These states could facilitate the acquisition of materials for making weapons of mass destruction or provide such weapons to terrorist groups. Rogue states also have the potential to pose more than an indirect threat. As ballistic missile delivery ranges increase and weapons proliferation continues, CSIS argues, "states potentially hostile to Canadian interests could ... strike Canada directly."[43]

ASSESSING THE THREAT

Thus, statements of the threat to North America above and below the forty-ninth parallel centre on the threat of international terrorism, the growing possibility of a terrorist attack using weapons of mass destruction, the risk of information warfare, the indirect rogue state threat to North America by virtue of support to terrorism, and the possibility of a direct rogue state missile attack on North America. These assessments, in turn, are a product of changing strategic options and motives in the more than decade and a half since the end of the Cold War. The literature on this is vast and growing, especially in the wake of 9/11, and my purpose here is merely to highlight the range of salient explanatory points as a basis for charting the way forward.

Strategic Options

International terrorists and rogue states – and their potential use of weapons of mass destruction, information warfare, and perhaps ballistic missiles – are often collectively termed "asymmetric threats."[44] Asymmetric threats, as defined by the Joint Chiefs of Staff, are those that target US weaknesses or vulnerabilities and do not operate according to conventional modes of behaviour. Incentives for US adversaries to seek asymmetrical approaches centre on the overwhelming superiority of America's conventional military capabilities, first displayed during the 1991 Gulf War and demonstrated more recently in Kosovo (1999), Afghanistan (2001), and Iraq (2003). These capabilities have convinced adversaries that they cannot contest American power on the conventional battlefield and must seek alternative strategic options. "The overwhelming disparity between US forces and those of any potential rival drives terrorist adversaries to the extremes of warfare – toward 'the suicide bomber or the nuclear device' as the best way to confront the United States."[45]

The strategic appeal of conducting asymmetric warfare emerged at a time when adversarial groups were presented with increased options as to where to establish their base of operations. The demise of the Soviet Union and the end of the Cold War brought an end to superpower support of many Third World regimes, inadvertently contributing to the emergence of the "failed state" phenomenon. Whereas previously such states were viewed as a humanitarian tragedy, 9/11 also revealed their potential to create major national security problems. The CIA has drawn attention to places like Somalia, where the absence of a national government has allowed Al Qaeda sympathizers to offer terrorists an operational base and a haven, and the lawless zone along the Afghanistan-Pakistan border, where extremist movements can find shelter and "the breathing space to grow."[46] A high-level bipartisan study has argued that weak states – stretching in a broad band from Central America to Africa to south and central Asia – pose one of the biggest twenty-first-century threats to the United States.[47] "We know from the events of September 11th," former DCI Tenet has argued, "that we can never again ignore a specific type of country: a country unable to control its own borders and internal territory, lacking the capacity to govern ... Such countries offer extremists a place to congregate in relative safety."[48]

Motives

While the notion of asymmetric warfare and the existence of failed states may point us towards strategic options, understanding current assessments of the threat to North America must go deeper to include an examination of possible motives and sources of grievances. There are a multitude, some dating back to recent years and decades and others originating in past centuries. The most broadly conceived perspective on the international terrorist threat to the United States, and indeed to the Western world in general, places it in the context of the historic confrontation between the Muslim and Christian religions. The struggle between Islam and Christendom, argues Princeton's Bernard Lewis, "has now lasted for some fourteen centuries. It began with the advent of Islam, in the seventh century ... and has consisted of a long series of attacks and counterattacks ... For the first thousand years Islam was advancing, Christendom in retreat and under threat. For the past three hundred years Islam has been on the defensive ... For some time now there has been a rising tide of rebellion against this Western paramountcy."[49] In this conceptualization, the West and Islam are locked in a prolonged struggle, defined over centuries; and the contemporary era, marked as it is by Western domination, constitutes the darkest era in the history of Islam.[50]

The historical context has also been articulated in more recent terms, beginning with the collapse of the Ottoman Empire at the end of World War I. At that time, the Arabic-speaking peoples who had been part of the Turkish-ruled empire sought to establish an independent Arab state, but instead the region was divided up into British and French colonial possessions. "The absorption of virtually the whole Muslim world into various European empires in the early 20th century," argues the *Economist*, "is not a good neighbourly story."[51] After World War II, the state of Israel was created, further driving a wedge between the Arab states. The result is that for more than eighty years Arabs and Muslims have been humiliated – the most humiliating moment of all being the Israeli defeat of the Arab nations in the 1967 Six-Day War.[52]

Other explanations date to contemporary policies of the West in general and the United States in particular. The 1991 Gulf War is an important benchmark not so much because of the conflict itself but because in its aftermath a large number of Western – especially US – military forces were stationed in the region to enforce the no-fly zones over Iraq. Thus, Osama Bin Laden's February 1998 declaration of jihad stated as a key grievance: "For more than seven years the United States is occupying the lands of Islam in the holiest of its territories, Arabia."[53] Al Qaeda wants the United States, and the West more generally, out of the Persian Gulf and the Middle East.[54] (The United States withdrew most of its military forces from Saudi Arabia immediately after the war in Iraq in 2003.)

A second contemporary explanation focuses on the Israeli-Palestinian conflict and the view that the United States has unduly supported Israel at the expense of the suffering Palestinian people. Although many Arab and Islamic leaders were quick to condemn the 9/11 attacks, Arab and Muslim opinion has remained sharply critical of US policy in the Middle East and the US's perceived one-sided approach to the conflict.[55] Yet when it comes to Al Qaeda itself, the grievance does not appear to be a long-standing one. In his 1998 statement Bin Laden did not devote significant attention to the conflict, and not until October 2001 did he focus his verbal wrath on Israel's occupation of Palestinian lands.[56] Moreover, experts have argued that certain historical discrepancies make it difficult to pinpoint American support for Israel as the single, simple cause of terrorist activity against the US. Soon after the founding of Israel the Soviet Union granted immediate de jure recognition and support, and yet there seems to have been no great ill will towards the Soviets for this.[57] Nonetheless, it is certainly true that the ongoing Israeli-Palestinian conflict forms one of Bin Laden's principal arguments for claiming that Western nations are aligned against Muslims.[58]

Some explanations centre on particular attributes of the United States and the West. "At times [Muslim] hatred goes beyond hostility to specific interests or actions or policies or even countries and becomes a rejection of Western civilization ... not only what its does but what it is, and the principles and values it practices and professes."[59] This is the explanation invoked most often by members of the Bush administration, who identify the source of the terrorist threat to North America as "the enemies of freedom" and their rejection of everything the West stands for. The perception is that the West represents a way of living that so fundamentally violates the will of God and offends traditional Islam that true believers have an obligation to bring it down.[60] Terrorists, goes this line of argument, hate America simply for what it is.[61]

Others argue that it is not so much that Muslim extremists are against everything the West stands for, but rather that with the demise of Communism and the ascendance of US power and culture in the post–Cold War system, the liberal-democratic way of life poses the most significant challenge to the alternative presented by Islam. Thus, Al Qaeda wants to purge the Middle East of American political, economic, and military power, but only as part of a far more sweeping religious agenda: a defensive jihad to defeat a rival system that poses an existential threat to Islam.[62]

It is also possible that policies, values, and ideological power politics have little to do with the sources of terrorism. The tangible record, argues one scholar, demonstrates that America's policies in the Middle East have been remarkably pro-Arab and pro-Muslim over the years, including in the post–Cold War era.[63] America has supported Muslims in Afghanistan against the Soviet Union, in Kuwait and Saudi Arabia against Iraq, in Bosnia against Serbia, in Pakistan against India, and in Turkey against Greece. Even its support of Israel has extended only to helping Israel survive Arab efforts to remove it from the map.[64] At the same time, although Islam and Christendom have clashed for centuries, there is little in the essence of Islam that predetermines its adherents to violent conflict with the West.[65] Of the civilizations listed by Samuel Huntington,[66] the Islamic and Western appear to have more in common with one another than with many of the others.[67]

A key source of international terrorism is seen to lie in the lack of representative governments in the Arab world, which produces, proportionally, by far the greatest number of terrorists among Islamic countries. Some argue that oligarchic regimes portray US policy as anti-Arab in order to divert their subjects' attention from the internal weaknesses that are their real problem. "Thus, rather than pushing for greater privatization, equality for women, democracy, civil society, freedom of speech [and] due process of law, the public focuses instead on hating the United States."[68] In this conceptualization the basic reason for the prevalence of anti-Americanism is that it has been a useful tool for radical rulers, revolutionaries, and even moderate regimes to build domestic support.

Others see an indirect causal link in which the lack of democracy facilitates terrorism by inhibiting economic development and stemming alternative means of political expression. A 2002 United Nations Development Programme (UNDP) report found that for the previous twenty years, income per capita in the twenty-two Arab countries was lower than anywhere else in the world, with the exception of Sub-Saharan Africa. The UNDP blames the high level of poverty on the survival of absolute autocracies, the holding of bogus elections, confusion between the executive and the judiciary, constraints on the media, and an intolerant social environment.[69] At the same time, statistics indicate that in societies struggling with poverty, the freedom to assemble and protest peacefully without interference from the government goes a long way towards providing an alternative to terrorism.[70] In this sense, poverty is not a source of terrorism; rather, it is a facilitating factor. The causal link is the discontent created when those living in a situation of economic deprivation are also politically oppressed and have no legitimate venue for voicing their views on their own affairs.

Western economists agree that the best way to break the cycle is to found political and economic institutions that can create opportunity.[71] Indeed, the implementation of good governance at the local, state, and regional levels in the Middle East is seen as imperative for addressing the sources of terrorism.[72] But it is the governments themselves that must undertake these structural changes, and the prospect seems unlikely, at least in the short to medium term. In the first instance, it is an open question whether church and state can be separated in the Islamic faith. For some, Islam is inconsistent with democracy; for others, there is sufficient wiggle room within the Koran for the two to coexist.[73] Equally fundamental is that for many in the Arab world, to adopt Western ways is to approach the problem backwards. Developmental failures are attributed not to a lack of democracy and modernization but rather to the Arab world having neglected Islam. Political Islam sees the solution as embracing Islam more fully and rejecting the ways of the West.[74]

Capabilities

The threat to North America reflects not only the motives and circumstances behind potential terrorists but also their increased means and capacity to present a significant danger. Weapons of mass destruction have proliferated among state actors over the past several years. For half a century weapon-design information and the technology for producing fissile material for nuclear weapons was the purview of only a few countries. But in 1998 India and Pakistan detonated nuclear bombs, in 2002 North Korea confirmed it had restarted its uranium enrichment program, and there continue to be strong concerns that Iran is developing nuclear weapons. Brazil has also announced that it will start enriching uranium and has rejected the more intrusive checks of the International Atomic Energy Agency, alarming Argentina, which, like Brazil, had a nascent nuclear program until 1991.[75] The United States believes that several other countries in addition to North Korea and Iran may be trying to develop nuclear weapons, although it has not revealed which ones.[76]

A major factor impacting nuclear proliferation was the demise of the Soviet Union, which resulted in looser controls on nuclear materials and created a large pool of unemployed scientists willing to sell their nuclear knowledge to other countries. Equally if not more damaging have been the actions of Abdul Qadeer Khan, the father of Pakistan's nuclear program. In 2004 it came to light that for a decade and a half he had run an underground network that supplied nuclear technology to countries like Iran, Libya, and North Korea. The head of the International Atomic Energy Agency has stated that up to forty countries are capable of manufacturing nuclear weapons within just a few months.[77]

Meanwhile, the US intelligence community estimates that about a dozen states maintain offensive biological warfare programs, as compared to the three or four that were thought to have offensive biological weapons programs when the Biological Weapons Convention entered into force in 1975. Iran, Syria, Libya, China, North Korea, Russia, Israel, Taiwan, and possibly Sudan, India, Pakistan, and Kazakhstan are all believed to possess biological weapons.[78] Prior to the 2003 war in Iraq the US intelligence community assessed that despite the Chemical Weapons Convention, at least sixteen states continued to maintain active, clandestine chemical weapons programs.[79]

Complicating an assessment of rogue-state WMD capabilities is the increased challenge of intelligence detection. Chemical and biological weapons programs have always been hard to detect because of the dual nature of the technology involved. But the CIA notes that it has become even more difficult to monitor maturing biological and chemical warfare programs in countries of concern, like Iran, North Korea, and Syria, because these countries are becoming less reliant on foreign suppliers. Indigenous biological warfare programs have become more technologically sophisticated as a result of a rapid growth in the field of biotechnology and the spread of information through the Internet.[80] Indeed, much of the latent ability of state and non-state actors to develop chemical, biological, and even nuclear weapons can be explained by the impact of economic, educational, and technological progress. "The new physics that Manhattan Project scientists had to discover to make nuclear weapons possible is now standard textbook fare for young physicists and engineers."[81]

Not only are WMD programs becoming more advanced but also countries of concern are becoming more aggressive in pursuing them. The desire for nuclear weapons is on the upsurge, argues the CIA, and additional countries may seek nuclear weapons as it becomes clear that their neighbours and regional rivals are doing so. But regional rivalry is not the only factor. The example of states, like North Korea, deterring far more powerful countries, like the United States, by virtue of possessing a nuclear weapon is likely to resonate strongly with other states struggling to contend with vast asymmetries in power.

There is significant evidence that terrorist organizations are attempting to acquire weapons of mass destruction. As early as 1998 Bin Laden publicly declared that acquiring unconventional weapons was "a religious duty."[82] Documents recovered from Al Qaeda facilities in Afghanistan in the fall of 2001 revealed that Al Qaeda's search for WMD had been even more determined, and had progressed even further, than was previously believed. Most notably, Al Qaeda was pursuing a sophisticated biological weapons research program focusing on a number of agents, including anthrax.[83] The CIA believes that Al Qaeda was also seeking to acquire or develop a nuclear device, and that it may be pursuing a radioactive dispersal device, or a "dirty bomb."[84]

Intelligence organizations continue to receive indications that Al Qaeda is seeking chemical, biological, radiological, and nuclear weapons. The Department of Homeland Security has stated that Al Qaeda is aggressively pursuing a WMD capability, and that the acquisition, production, or theft of such weapons remains a top Al Qaeda objective.[85] CSIS has concluded that whether or not Al Qaeda actually has "briefcase-sized" nuclear weapons, there is no doubt that the terrorist network is intent on acquiring nuclear capabilities.[86] A United Nations panel has concluded that the Al Qaeda network would like to use chemical and biological weapons but does not yet have the technological expertise to do so,[87] while the head of the International Atomic Energy Agency has bluntly warned of the imminent danger of terrorists acquiring nuclear materials.[88] Particular concern centres on the acquisition of biological weapons, since these weapons combine maximum destructiveness with easy availability.[89] As is the case with rogue-state actors, the increased dissemination of information is instrumental in assessing the means and capacities of terrorist organizations. Today, terrorist groups worldwide have ready access to information on chemical, biological, and even nuclear weapons.

Increased means and capacities involve not only the destructive device itself but also the delivery vehicle – generally, ballistic missile technology. Whereas only eight countries were capable of fielding ballistic missiles in 1972, that number has since grown to twenty-five, according to the Pentagon's Missile Defence Agency.[90]

Most of these nations are in the Middle East or Asia. In the CIA's view, the proliferation of intercontinental ballistic missiles and cruise missiles has raised the threat to the US from WMD delivery systems to a critical threshold.

Long-range ballistic missiles are sufficiently imprecise that they do not present a significant danger in the hands of a hostile force unless the missile has a nuclear or biological warhead.[91] For this reason it is imperative to identify those actors seeking to acquire both long-range missiles and a WMD capability. As mentioned earlier, the source of greatest concern is North Korea, which beyond its nuclear program is also reportedly using Russian technology to develop the Taepo Dong-2 missile, with a range of up to 15,000 kilometres, far enough to reach all locations on the west coast of the United States and – in theory, at least – any target on US soil.[92] Iran is also expected to develop an intercontinental ballistic missile capability by the end of the decade.[93] Despite these intelligence assessments, however, there are still large gaps in US knowledge about how advanced North Korean and Iranian intercontinental ballistic missile efforts may be.[94]

Just as ballistic missile technology is proliferating, so other methods of delivering weapons of mass destruction are becoming apparent. State and non-state actors are no longer limited to traditional methods, such as bombers and sophisticated ballistic missiles. They can now transport highly destructive devices in small trucks, cargo containers, boats, and airplanes. Thus, weapons of mass destruction, and especially nuclear and biological weapons, are dangerous even in the absence of ballistic missiles.

Although WMD terrorism dominates contemporary debate in academic and official circles over threats to North America, some experts are careful to put the threats in perspective by pointing out the technical difficulties involved in conducting terrorist attacks with chemical and biological weapons. Carrying out a terrorist attack with chemical weapons is not an easy task. It takes massive amounts of a chemical agent to produce significant casualties, and the agent itself, being highly susceptible to wind patterns, is hard to disseminate with any precision. The technical challenges of using biological agents to produce massive fatalities are also daunting in that lethal doses must be inhaled, and the particles involved must be of a particular size (not too small to be exhaled and not too large to be blocked before reaching the lungs).[95]

The relative difficulty of deploying weapons of mass destruction indicates that in the majority of cases terrorists will likely continue to choose simpler conventional methods, such as hijackings and bombings. Only in a very few cases have terrorist groups been able to amass the skills, knowledge, material, and equipment to perpetrate attacks with unconventional weapons on a scale equal to that of conventional methods.[96] Nonetheless, it is the one attack of this nature that officials fear the most. Studies have shown, for example, that a single airplane delivering one hundred kilograms of anthrax spores by aerosol on a clear, calm night over Washington, DC, could cause more than a million casualties.[97] WMD terrorism is a high-consequence, low-probability (but growing) threat that, based on the changing nature of terrorism, is the greatest contemporary hazard facing North America.

CONCLUSION

Thus, an assessment of the threat to North America points to the strategic option of asymmetric warfare, the vast range of plausible sources and motivations behind such activity, and the growing capabilities of the actors involved. The list of issues is no doubt partial, and the discussion admittedly cursory. But it does reveal a crucial element of the threat to North America: while it may be possible to reduce the threat through policy adjustments or changes in approach, in the final analysis it cannot be eliminated in the short to medium term. Like it or not, "The world is becoming more religious, religious expression is generally becoming more assertive and apocalyptic thinking more prominent. Weapons of mass destruction, spectacularly suited to cosmic war, are becoming more widely available."[98] There are some encouraging signs of democracy in the Middle East, but this development is still in its earliest stages. Ultimately, Canada and the United States will need to defend themselves offensively and defensively, and through some combination of civilian and military measures, against the primary threat of international terrorism, as well as against other threats. The challenge is to find and undertake the necessary balance of activities. But first it is useful to take a step back and examine America's understanding of, and approach to, the threat to North America as it emerged in the first post–Cold War decade.

3

The Evolution of US Security and Defence Policy in the Post–Cold War Era

The essence of an asymmetric threat is the notion of using unconventional means, such as terrorism and/or weapons of mass destruction, to target the perceived vulnerabilities and weaknesses of a more powerful actor. Although US military forces and civilian facilities overseas do face asymmetric threats, throughout the 1990s defence analysts within and outside the US government increasingly voiced their concern that a key area of weakness was the nation's ability to protect itself at home. A tragic validation of this argument occurred on 11 September 2001.

This chapter traces the evolution of the US government's understanding of the asymmetric threat in the post–Cold War era by examining America's key security and defence policy statements, as well as reports by high-level bipartisan commissions, during the administrations of Bill Clinton and George W. Bush. What emerges is a picture of officials making increasingly prophetic predictions of the calamity to come. Moreover, it becomes apparent that despite the dramatic change in the North American security environment, US security strategy remains as firmly rooted in the overseas dimension of protecting American soil as it was during the Cold War.

THE CLINTON ADMINISTRATION

Bottom-Up Review

The first full post–Cold War statement of US defence policy was the Clinton administration's *Bottom-Up Review* (BUR), released in

May 1993. While the term "asymmetric warfare" does not appear in it, the review does cover aspects of the security environment that would later be associated with the asymmetric threat to North America. The BUR notes that the most striking aspect of the transition from the Cold War to the post–Cold War era was the dramatic shift in the nature of the dangers to America's interests. The previous global threat from massive Soviet nuclear and conventional forces had been replaced, it argues, by myriad smaller "dangers." Number one on the list is the dangers posed by nuclear weapons and other weapons of mass destruction, including those associated with the proliferation of nuclear, biological, and chemical weapons, and with the large stockpiles of these weapons remaining in the former Soviet Union.[1]

Beyond this brief mention of proliferation and WMD in the opening section of the BUR, however, there is no further elaboration. There is no discussion of how US military strategy might be adjusted in light of these threats; nor is there any attempt to place the proliferation of WMD in the context of threats to the US homeland. The focus is on the need to project power into regions important to US interests and to defeat two potentially hostile regional powers, such as North Korea and Iraq, in overlapping time frames. In the BUR defending the United States remains very much something that is done overseas. The idea that threats might arise from within the continent is beyond its conceptual boundaries, as is any notion of viewing such threats collectively in terms of their asymmetric nature.

Joint Vision 2010

The first official US defence policy document to make specific reference to the concept of asymmetric warfare was *Joint Vision 2010*, released by the chairman of the Joint Chiefs of Staff in June 1996. America's "most vexing future adversary," the document states, "may be one who can use … asymmetrical counters to U.S. military strengths." These adversaries "will have an independent will, some knowledge of our capabilities, and a desire to avoid our strengths and exploit our vulnerabilities."[2] Despite this insight, potential adversaries continue to be discussed in terms of their threat to overseas situations, not to the US homeland. The emphasis is on wider access to advanced technology and weapons of

mass destruction, and the impact this will have on the number of
actors with sufficient military potential to upset existing regional
balances of power.

Quadrennial Defense Review of 1997

The 1997 *Quadrennial Defense Review* (QDR) is the first post–Cold
War US defence policy document to mesh the idea of asymmetric
warfare with threats to North America. In its opening discussion
of the global security environment, the review highlights a range
of significant challenges to US security in the period to 2015.
These include the by now familiar regional dangers, like rogue
states, and the proliferation of weapons of mass destruction, which
could destabilize regions and increase the number of adversaries
with significant military capabilities. In a departure from the
Bottom-Up Review, the 1997 *Quadrennial Defense Review* also draws
attention to the phenomena of failed states and the role they could
play in creating instability, as well as to transnational dangers like
the illegal drug trade, international organized crime, and terrorism. "Increasingly capable and violent terrorists," the QDR argues,
"will continue to directly threaten the lives of American citizens
[overseas] and try to undermine U.S. policies and alliances." The
review's final observation about the global security environment
is that while the United States is "dramatically safer than during
the Cold War, the U.S. homeland is not free from external threats."
This refers in part to the latent threat posed by the strategic
nuclear arsenals of Russia and China. In addition, "other unconventional means of attack, such as terrorism, are no longer just
threats to our diplomats and military forces overseas, but will
threaten Americans at home in the years to come."[3]

Thus the QDR of 1997 went directly to the notion of asymmetric
threats to the US homeland. This, as we have seen, was a completely new area of focus for official US defence policy in the post–
Cold War era. The document argues that US dominance in the
conventional military arena could encourage adversaries to use
"asymmetric" means – defined in the document as "unconventional
approaches to circumvent or undermine our strengths while exploit-
ing our vulnerabilities" – to attack forces and interests overseas and
Americans at home. "Strategically," the review goes on to explain,
"an aggressor may seek to avoid direct military confrontation

with the United States, using means such as terrorism, NBC threats, information warfare, or environmental sabotage instead in order to achieve its goals."[4]

Although the 1997 QDR identified the asymmetric threat to the US homeland, it made no attempt to determine how the United States might respond to it. The review pointed out that US forces overseas were also likely to face asymmetric threats, and that dealing with such asymmetric challenges should be an important part of US defence strategy, from fielding new capabilities to changing how US forces operate in future contingencies. However, it did not address how the US military might deal with asymmetric threats to the homeland. The major force-sizing framework contained in the QDR of 1997 continued to be that which was established in the Bottom-Up Review – namely, the ability to "deter and defeat large-scale, cross-border aggression in two distant theatres in overlapping time frames."[5]

National Defense Panel

Developing a homeland response to asymmetric threats was one of the key gaps in analysis that was identified in a December 1997 report by a bipartisan commission of experts called the National Defense Panel. Created by Congress in 1996 to give a parallel and independent assessment of the ongoing QDR, the panel put forward a number of ideas that proved to be remarkably prescient and remain highly relevant today. Its report, entitled *Transforming Defense: National Security in the 21st Century*, was the first high-level US defence and security policy document in the post–Cold War era to highlight and emphasize the need to take measures to defend the US homeland from asymmetric threats. "We can assume that our enemies and our adversaries have learned from the Gulf War," the report states. "They are unlikely to confront us conventionally … [Rather] they will look for ways to match their strengths against our weaknesses. In short, we can expect those opposed to our interests to confront us at home and abroad – possibly in both places at once – with asymmetrical responses to our traditional strengths."[6]

This is not to say that the report focuses entirely on the US homeland – far from it. It also stresses the overseas dimension of protecting the United States, and one of its key criticisms of the

1997 *QDR* is that the review did not adequately address the need to transform US military forces for the power projection requirements of the future. As well, the report deals at length with the nature of the asymmetric threat to military forces abroad – such as enemies blocking US access to overseas ports by threatening to use (or actually deploying) weapons of mass destruction.

But *Transforming Defense* was a trailblazing document in that it gave at least equal weight to the asymmetric threat to the homeland and the role of the military in confronting that threat. The panel predicted that enemies would use terror as a weapon against America's will; terrorist attacks would compel the US to divert assets to protect critical infrastructures and populations at home. Weapons of mass destruction, especially, were identified by the panel as a serious and growing threat to the people of the United States. Examples include chemical and biological weapons used on mass-transportation systems and small nuclear devices smuggled into population centres. These developments, the report argues, would require a military response. "Just as deployments abroad are key to a stable international environment, an adequate defensive structure at home is crucial to the safety of [US] citizens ... One of the salient features of U.S. security in 2010–2020 will be a much larger role for homeland defense than exists today."[7]

Transforming Defense ranked homeland defence as America's number-one national security challenge – above regional stability and power projection – in the period to 2020. Besides an ongoing need to deter a strategic nuclear attack, it argued, the United States had a need to defend itself against terrorism, information warfare, weapons of mass destruction, ballistic and cruise missiles, and other transnational threats to its sovereign territory. In many cases civilian agencies would have to take the lead in responding to an asymmetric homeland threat, but the US military would also play a key role in some missions. Moreover, the military had to be prepared to play an active role in supporting the civilian agencies.

Among the National Defense Panel's recommendations were:

- The America's Command be created to address the challenges of homeland defence (today we see this in the new Northern Command);
- A missile defence system be deployed that is capable of defeating limited ballistic missile attacks;

- Passive and active defence measures be developed against the use of WMD;
- National Guard units – although kept as an overseas reserve – be given additional specific training to assist in responding to civil emergencies, including the WMD threat and information warfare, and even assisting in national missile defence;
- Military capabilities be called upon to assist in protecting the nation from threats such as cyber-terrorism on America's information or economic infrastructures;
- Changes be made to the intelligence structure to eliminate artificial bureaucratic boundaries that prevent the timely sharing of information; and
- The entire US national security structure, which dated from 1947, be re-examined. (Coordination gaps among US government agencies, the report argued, would impede US domestic-crisis response capabilities.)

It is evident from this list that the panel proposed changes that pertained not only to the US military but also to the entire US security structure and key civilian agencies within that structure. The panel anticipated many of the problems that were exposed by 9/11, and elements of many of its recommendations are now being implemented.

National Security Strategy for a New Century

The National Defense Panel's strong emphasis on threats to the US homeland was partially reflected in the next major US security policy document, *National Security Strategy for a New Century*, released by the White House National Security Council in October 1998. In its preface, the document presented a "forward-looking national security strategy attuned to the realities of our new era."[8] The strategy's three core objectives were to enhance US security, to bolster America's economic prosperity, and to promote democracy abroad. To these ends the strategy encompassed a wide range of initiatives, like expanding NATO, working with Ukraine and Russia, promoting free trade through the World Trade Organization, promoting arms control regimes, and developing multinational coalitions to combat terrorism. Surprisingly, measures to increase homeland security and defence are entirely absent from this opening list. Only later, after mentioning things like "renewing a commitment to America's diplomacy," does the document state, "Protecting U.S. citizens and critical infrastructures at home is an essential element of U.S. strategy."[9]

The document's discussion of threats to US interests gives greater attention to homeland threats. Second on the list, after regional or state-centred threats, is transnational threats, including the possibility that terrorists could target the US homeland directly with weapons of mass destruction or target US infrastructure with an information warfare attack. Based on this assessment, *National Security Strategy for a New Century* highlights a number of initiatives that were underway at that time to address the increased asymmetric threat to the homeland:

- Presidential Decision Directive 62 on combatting terrorism was signed in May 1998. It established an overarching policy and assigned responsibilities for responding to terrorist acts on US soil involving WMD;
- The Domestic Terrorism Program was building a capability in 120 major US cities for first-responders to deal with WMD incidents. The Department of Defense (DoD) was (and continues to be) heavily involved in training these first-responders;
- In May 1998 President Clinton announced that DoD would train Army National Guard and reserve elements to assist state and local authorities in consequence management;
- Also in May, the president announced a comprehensive strategy to protect the civilian population from biological weapons, including upgrading the public health and medical surveillance systems, training first-responders, stockpiling vaccines, and increasing research and development into new vaccines and medicines;
- Presidential Decision Directive 63 on critical infrastructure protection, also signed in May 1998, made it US policy to take all necessary measures to eliminate significant vulnerabilities to physical or information attacks on US critical infrastructures, especially information systems;
- The directive provided for the creation of a national organizational structure to handle the cyber-threat, including sector coordinators to promote co-operation within industry, lead agencies to serve as conduits from government to each sector,

and the Office of National Infrastructure Assurance, associated
with the National Security Council;
- Beyond this, the Attorney General/FBI had established the
National Infrastructure Protection Center to integrate information
from federal, state, and local government entities, as well as the
private sector, on possible threats to national infrastructures.

Despite this flurry of activity, America's ability to cope with a
threat to the US homeland did not appreciably increase. Experts
faulted the government for having no coherent national strategy
for combatting terrorism and for having a multitude of programs
that were fragmented, uncoordinated, and politically unaccount-
able. The result was the creation in 1999 of another high-level
commission, the U.S. Commission on National Security/21st Century. Led by Senators Gary Hart and Warren Rudman, the commission met for two years and produced three reports. It sounded
even louder alarm bells than did the National Defense Panel, and
it produced even more prescient conclusions.

U.S. Commission on National Security/21st Century

The commission's number-one conclusion in its phase 1 report of
September 1999, entitled *New World Coming*, was that America
would "become increasingly vulnerable to hostile attack on its
homeland" and that US military superiority could not fully protect
the country from such attack. "American influence will increasingly be both embraced and resented abroad," it argued, "as U.S.
cultural, economic, and political power persists. States, terrorists,
and other disaffected groups will acquire weapons of mass destruction and mass disruption, and some will use them. *Americans will
likely die on American soil, possibly in large numbers.*"[10]

Based on this new security environment the commission's phase
2 report, *Seeking a National Strategy*, released in April 2000, attempts
to set out a coherent national security strategy for dealing with
the dangers ahead. It begins by pointing out that ten years after
the fall of the Berlin Wall, US national security strategy continued
to be derived largely from the measures drawn up shortly after
World War II to contain Soviet Communism. The structure had
not been altered because the United States had been victorious in
the Cold War, and serious reform rarely takes place in countries

that have not suffered a major defeat. Yet "Americans are less secure than they believe themselves to be. The time for re-examination is now, before the American people find themselves shocked by events they never anticipated."[11]

The first objective of a new national security strategy, the commission argued, should be to take measures to defend the United States and ensure that it was safe from the dangers of a new era – particularly those arising from the proliferation of weapons of mass destruction and terrorism. To this end, it stated, key policy aims must include:

- Building national defences against a limited ballistic missile attack;
- Developing methods to defend against other, covert means of attacking the United States with weapons of mass destruction and disruption (that is, information warfare);
- Considering carefully the means and circumstances of preemption; and
- Augmenting US public health capabilities to deal medically and psychologically with potentially large losses of American life in attacks against the American homeland.

The commission's third report, *Road Map for National Security*, released early in 2001, outlined the concrete organizational changes required to fulfill the proposed national security strategy. Not surprisingly, measures to secure the national homeland are first and foremost. "The combination of unconventional weapons proliferation with the persistence of international terrorism will end the relative invulnerability of the U.S. homeland to catastrophic attack," the report argues. "A direct attack against American citizens *on American soil* is likely over the next quarter century."[12] The commission therefore recommended the creation of an independent national homeland security agency with responsibility for planning, coordinating, and integrating various US government activities related to homeland security. The agency would be built upon the Federal Emergency Management Agency, which had primary responsibility for the consequence management of any WMD attack. The three organizations on the front line of border security – the Coast Guard, the Customs Service, and the Border

Patrol – would be transferred to the new agency. Dismissed as overly ambitious in early 2001, all of these recommendations have now been implemented in the context of the new Department of Homeland Security, the legislation for which was passed by Congress in December 2002.

THE BUSH ADMINISTRATION

Quadrennial Defence Review of 2001

The next major security policy statement released in the United States was the 2001 *Quadrennial Defense Review,* issued at the end of September 2001, about two and a half weeks after the terrorist attacks. The timing of the document's release, which had been set months in advance, necessitated many hasty revisions that could only partially accommodate the dramatic change in the international security environment. The section on defence strategy outlines four defence policy goals that are meant to provide "a new strategic framework to defend the nation and secure a viable peace."[13] Focused on the overseas element of defending the homeland, these goals include assuring allies and friends, dissuading future military competition, deterring threats and coercion against US interests, and, if deterrence fails, decisively defeating any adversary.

The force-planning priorities of the 2001 QDR are more directly reflective of the post-9/11 security environment. Appropriately titled "Paradigm Shift in Force Planning," this section of the document replaces the long-standing requirement to respond to two major regional contingencies with the less ambitious goal of achieving decisive victory in one regional conflict while containing another. More notably for our purposes here, however, the new force-sizing framework specifically shapes forces to defend the United States. This is number one on the defence planning list, followed by deterring regional aggression, defeating regional aggression, and conducting smaller scale contingency operations. In this way the framework "places new emphasis on the unique operational demands associated with the defense of the United States and restores the defense of the United States as the Department's primary mission."[14] Thus, although it is not stated as a defence policy goal, the direct defence of the United States figures prominently in the review's force-planning section. "The highest priority of the U.S. military," states the QDR of 2001, "is to defend the Nation from all enemies."[15] To this end the United States will maintain sufficient military forces to protect the US domestic population, its territory, and its critical defence-related infrastructure against attacks emanating from outside its borders.

Here the review makes implicit reference to a key issue with respect to homeland security and defence: what role the military should play when threats to the homeland emanate from within US borders rather than from outside them. This issue has recurred in the US homeland defence policy debate. It was raised by both the National Defense Panel and the U.S. Commission on National Security/21st Century, the latter arguing that new priorities had to be set for the US armed forces in light of the threat to the homeland. The commission recommended that the National Guard be given homeland security as a primary mission, but to date that recommendation has not been acted upon (see chapter 5).

National Security Strategy of the United States

Released in September 2002, the Bush administration's *National Security Strategy of the United States* places a greater emphasis on the US homeland than any previous official US defence or security policy document of the post–Cold War era. "Enemies in the past," President Bush points out in his opening letter, "needed great armies and great industrial capabilities to endanger America. Now, shadowy networks of individuals can bring great chaos and suffering to our shores for less than it costs to purchase a single tank."[16] To defeat this threat, Bush continues, the United States must make use of every tool in its arsenal: military power, better homeland defences, law enforcement, intelligence, and vigorous efforts to cut off terrorist financing. Several of these clearly centre on the homeland element of bringing security to America. The strategy also emphasizes the need to strengthen America's intelligence on threats emanating from within the country that are inspired by foreign governments and groups.

Beyond these points, however, America's new national security strategy remains rooted in the overseas dimension of guaranteeing security for the US homeland. Although it recognizes the need to increase America's homeland security in order to protect against and deter attack, the strategy takes as its basic starting point the notion that the "best defence is a good offence." The overseas-oriented defence policy goals of the 2001 QDR are reiterated verbatim, and the bulk of the *National Security Strategy* centres on things like:

- Strengthening alliances to defeat global terrorism;
- Identifying and destroying the terrorist threat before it reaches America's borders;
- Investing time and resources in building international relationships;
- Developing co-operative agendas with other main centres of global power; and
- Stopping rogue states before they can threaten the United States and its allies with WMD.

When it comes to military responses to the threat, the *National Security Strategy* raises two possibilities: deterrence and pre-emptive action. The former is quickly dismissed as not being a viable option. The nature of the threat, the document argues, has fundamentally changed in the post–Cold War era, especially since 9/11. During the Cold War the United States faced a generally status quo, risk-adverse opponent. "But deterrence based only on the threat of retaliation is less likely to work against leaders of rogue states more willing to take risks, gambling with the lives of their people."[17] The *National Security Strategy* goes on to note that during the Cold War, weapons of mass destruction were considered weapons of last resort that could destroy those who used them. Yet today they may be considered weapons of choice in the face of overwhelming US conventional superiority. Moreover, if traditional concepts of deterrence do not work on rogue regimes, then they are even less applicable to international terrorists who have no state or territory to defend, and who include suicide as an operational strategy.

If not deterrence, then what? When it comes to military responses, the *National Security Strategy*'s answer is pre-emptive military action. The document notes that for centuries, legal scholars conditioned the legitimacy of pre-emption on the existence of an imminent threat, most often a visible mobilization of armies, navies, and air forces in preparation for an attack. But the nature of the threat today – involving rogue states, terrorists, and weapons that can be easily concealed, delivered covertly, and used without warning – is such that there can be an imminent threat without visible warning. Moreover, the weapons involved may be weapons of mass destruction. Therefore, "as a matter of common sense and self-defense, America will act against such emerging threats before they are fully formed."[18] Although the strategy refers to this idea as the pre-emptive use of force (against an imminent or proximate threat), in fact the more accurate term when describing an emerging threat is "preventive war" (against a non-imminent or non-proximate threat).[19]

Relaxing the traditional requirements of necessity and imminence creates a potentially destabilizing precedent by making it possible for powerful countries to intervene wherever and whenever they choose. Yet we must recognize that today the threats are very different from what they were when international law on pre-emptive war was first developed.[20] The law was sufficient when the context was conventional threats against states; however, in an era when the primary concern is the terrorist use of WMD, waiting until the threat is apparent will not generally allow enough time to mobilize an effective defence.

In the report of the High-Level Panel on Threats, Challenges and Change, the United Nations attempted to adapt the concept of imminent threat to contemporary circumstances. Taking its cue from the doctrine of just war, the report reaffirms the right of pre-emptive use of force and expands the right of anticipatory self-defence to include preventive war, as long as certain conditions are met. These include proper purpose (or right intention), last resort, proportional means, and balance of consequences (or reasonable prospect of success). But the crucial, and most intangible, criterion is seriousness of threat. "Is the threatened harm to the State of a kind, and sufficiently clear and serious, to justify prima facie the use of military force?"[21] In other words, is there just cause? Establishing thresholds for this question would have gone to the heart of determining when it is legitimate to act against today's perceived potential threats; unfortunately, the UN does not attempt to do so. That said, one of the report's principal authors does provide some guidance: "It may be that there is nothing much to be gained by attempts at further refinement ... What matters is that the question be asked, and given a rational and credible answer."[22]

CONCLUSION

An examination of major American security statements from the 1990s reveals a growing and almost prophetic anticipation of the nature of events to come, particularly on the part of the independent, bipartisan commissions. Early documents from the 1990s made almost no reference to the US homeland, while those appearing later in the decade increasingly focused on the asymmetric threat to America at home. Nonetheless, the change in the nature of the threat has not appreciably changed America's approach to addressing threats. Although there has been a greater emphasis on defensive measures, particularly in the wake of 9/11, official US policy remains almost as firmly entrenched in the overseas dimension of defending North America as it was during the Cold War.

Is this an appropriate emphasis? "Because of its geography the United States has become accustomed to defending its borders offensively abroad," one scholar has argued. "But in this battle the defensive will loom equally large, if not larger."[23] Finding the right balance between the offence and the defence necessarily involves a closer look at the civilian and military components, both at home and abroad, of guaranteeing North American security. The next chapter examines the first part of this four-part framework: civilian measures at home – that is, homeland security.

4

Homeland Security

"Homeland security" refers to civilian-led measures to protect the people, property, and systems of a country. In enacting these measures the military could play a supporting role to a civilian agency, or it could play no role at all. "Homeland defence" is a subset of the overarching homeland security concept and refers to military-led measures to defend a national territory.[1] This chapter provides an overview of the numerous homeland security initiatives that have been taken jointly or separately by the United States and Canada since 11 September 2001, while chapter 5 focuses on homeland defence issues. Both chapters examine areas of ongoing contention or debate and propose some solutions.

HOMELAND SECURITY IN THE UNITED STATES

The Department of Homeland Security

In December 2002 President Bush signed into law legislation to fold 170,000 employees and 22 agencies into the Department of Homeland Security. The creation of the department, which formally came into existence in March 2003, represents the biggest US government reorganization since 1947. Prior to its creation there were a multitude of US departments and agencies – forty-four, by most counts – that played some role in various aspects of homeland security. The 11 September attacks highlighted the need to integrate these functions. Within a month of the attacks this task was assigned to the newly created Cabinet-level Office of Homeland

Security. But because it lacked a budget and direct resources, the office proved incapable of coordinating the agencies.[2] Congressional pressure on the president to create a department of homeland security mounted throughout the winter and spring of 2002, and he responded by presenting a draft blueprint for the department in June 2002. Although congressional-presidential wrangling over the details prevented any final decisions from being made until after the November 2002 mid-term elections, the end product closely followed the president's original blueprint.

The Department of Homeland Security has four major directorates. The Border and Transportation Security Directorate is the largest, and it has been given the mandate of securing America's borders, transportation systems, and territorial waters. To ensure the security of US borders the directorate has assumed authority over the Customs Service; the Immigration and Naturalization Service and its primary enforcement unit, the Border Patrol; and the Animal and Plant Health Inspection Service. In the area of transportation the directorate has incorporated the Transportation Security Administration, created after 9/11 as a component of the Department of Transport to ensure the security of America's transportation systems, including airports, railways, and transit systems. The US Coast Guard, with its enforcement role in securing territorial waters, was transferred from the Department of Transportation to the Department of Homeland Security. Although the commandant of the Coast Guard reports directly to the homeland security secretary, the Coast Guard also works closely with the Border and Transportation Security Directorate and reports to the secretary of defense in times of war.

The second directorate is that of Emergency Preparedness and Response, with responsibility for ensuring that the United States is prepared for, and can recover from, a terrorist attack or natural disaster. This is often referred to as "consequence management" – dealing with the aftermath of a homeland security incident. In the event of a major incident, the department would coordinate the involvement of other federal response assets, such as the National Guard. The core of this directorate is the Federal Emergency Management Agency (FEMA), formerly an independent agency. The third directorate, Science and Technology, coordinates the department's efforts in research and development. It focuses

especially on chemical, biological, radiological, and nuclear coun-
termeasures for use in the event of a terrorist attack involving
weapons of mass destruction.

Finally, the Information Analysis and Infrastructure Protection
Directorate is responsible for integrating intelligence and information pertaining to threats to the homeland from multiple sources,
assessing this information, issuing the necessary warnings, and
taking preventive measures. The sources include the Central
Intelligence Agency (CIA), Federal Bureau of Investigation (FBI),
National Security Agency, Immigration and Naturalization Service, Drug Enforcement Administration, Department of Energy,
Customs, and Department of Transportation. Prior to the establishment of the Department of Homeland Security, the US government had no institution primarily dedicated to analyzing all
information and intelligence on potential terrorist threats within
the United States (a task that the CIA performs in relation to terrorist threats abroad). This fourth directorate is also responsible
for evaluating the vulnerabilities of America's critical infrastructures – such as nuclear power plants, water facilities, and telecommunications networks – and taking the lead in coordinating federal,
state, and local efforts to protect the infrastructure. Although there
can be physical threats to critical infrastructures, one of the biggest concerns is a computer-network or cyber-attack on essential
services. Therefore, the directorate also unifies the various cyber-
security activities previously performed by other departments,
including the White House.[3]

The Department of Homeland Security is a work in progress,
and it will likely be years before its various entities are integrated
into an efficient organization. Some of the early difficulties originated in the lack of clear guidelines on specific roles and mandates
of organizations within the department, while others pertained to
the relationship of this huge new federal government department
to established departments like the Department of State.[4] But
probably the greatest challenges lie in the area of intelligence.
Although information analysis is one of the department's four
core functions, the main US intelligence agencies, the FBI and the
CIA, remain separate from the Department of Homeland Security.
In fact, roughly 80 per cent of the US intelligence establishment,
in terms of functions and resources, has historically been located
in the Department of Defense (DoD).[5] As a result, there is no

guarantee that the Department of Homeland Security will receive all of the intelligence it needs to conduct its analysis.

The creation of a Cabinet-level intelligence position may go some way towards resolving this problem. The National Commission on Terrorist Attacks upon the United States (the 9/11 Commission) found that two of the key factors behind the failure to prevent the 9/11 attacks were a lack of intelligence-sharing among government agencies and the fact that individual agencies did not rate specific information important enough to pass up the chain of command to the National Security Council.[6] Therefore, the commission recommended the creation of a national intelligence director position with budgetary authority over all of the federal government's intelligence agencies. The director would be responsible for ensuring that the relevant organizations focused on the right threats and sent information on to those who need it.[7] President Bush moved rapidly to win acceptance for the idea of a national intelligence director, and, significantly – despite concerns in the Pentagon – he also agreed to give the position power over budgets. This was important: the 9/11 Commission found that in 1998 DCI George Tenet recognized the seriousness of the threat posed by Al Qaeda but did not have the budgetary authority to direct resources where he believed they were needed.[8] Indeed, without substantial budget authority it is hard to see how the role of national intelligence director would differ much from that of DCI, a position created with the *National Security Act* of 1947 to coordinate planning and resource allocation among US intelligence agencies. The intelligence reform bill, signed into law at the end of 2004, created the new post of director of national intelligence with budgetary authority over all US intelligence agencies (but not over battlefield assets, of which the Pentagon retains control).

Homeland Security Initiatives

Since its creation the Department of Homeland Security has been very active in all of the sea, land, and air dimensions of homeland security. One of its biggest concerns is that a chemical, biological, or radiological weapon could be smuggled into a US port in one of the thousands of cargo containers that arrive every day. Aside from its lethal effects, the explosion of a biological, chemical, or radiological weapon in a US port could have a severe impact on the US economy. In light of this, the department has undertaken the Container Security Initiative, which involves US inspectors stationed at foreign ports using an automated system to analyze manifests and identify high-risk containers so that they can be more closely inspected. The first phase of the initiative involved twenty large container ports in Europe and Asia; the second phase has focused on major seaports in selected Muslim nations.[9] As part of the initiative, vessels headed for the United States are required to transmit their cargo manifests to US authorities before they even leave the foreign port, allowing customs officials to better track high-risk cargo containers. Since April 2005 Canadian border agents have also been deployed at foreign ports to help the United States search shipping containers bound for North America.[10]

Closer to home, the US Coast Guard has been assigned many homeland security tasks in the area of port protection. Before 9/11 these tasks were not very demanding; since the attacks they have absorbed some 30 per cent of the Coast Guard's operating time. This has raised questions as to whether the Coast Guard can juggle the new requirements with its ongoing responsibility for patrolling territorial waters and apprehending smugglers.[11] Even bigger questions have been raised about the ability of the Coast Guard to maintain its third mission area: participating as an integral part of the US military's overseas operations. The Pentagon has considered relieving the Coast Guard of its long-standing war-fighting role so it can focus on its homeland security tasks along domestic coastlines, but increased funding appears to have forestalled any mandate change by enabling the Coast Guard to devote adequate resources to all three missions.[12]

Notwithstanding the increased emphasis on port security, many are concerned that not enough is being done. Experts note that although the CIA has concluded that weapons of mass destruction would most likely enter the United States by sea, "the federal government is spending more every three days to finance the war in Iraq than it has provided over the past three years to prop up the security of all 361 US commercial seaports."[13] Of the 20,000 containers that enter US ports every day, only about 5 per cent are inspected.[14] More broadly, two years after 9/11 an independent task force chaired by one of the authors of the reports of the US Commission on National Security/21st Century found that America remained "dangerously ill-prepared to handle a catastrophic incident on American soil."[15]

For increased security on land, including at North American ports, much of what the United States is doing on its northern border is in the context of the Canada-US Smart Border Agreement, to be discussed later. Beyond this, the US Border Patrol has tripled the number of enforcement officers assigned to the Canada-US border (including the Alaska stretch) to over 1,000 agents. Although large, this number is still far smaller than the close to 10,000 officers assigned to the US-Mexico border.[16] The United States is also creating five bases across the northern United States from which to launch helicopters, airplanes, and high-speed boats to patrol for illegal border crossings.[17] The intelligence reform bill signed in December 2004 requires the Department of Homeland Security to increase the number of border patrol agents on America's northern and southern borders by a total of 10,000 over five years.

One way in which the United States is seeking to improve monitoring of its northern and, especially, southern land borders is by employing unmanned aerial vehicles (UAVs). It has already allocated billions of dollars to the development of UAVs for homeland security missions along its borders and coasts. The Coast Guard, for example, plans to use UAVs to help patrol the waters around the United States. Depending on feasibility, as well as on the resolution of certain safety and privacy issues, other potential homeland missions for unmanned aerial vehicles include monitoring oil and gas pipelines, electricity transmission lines, power plants, dams and drinking water supplies, and transportation routes for hazardous materials.[18] It is possible that within the next few years the Department of Homeland Security will be a bigger customer of unmanned aerial vehicles than the Pentagon.[19] Before then, however, it will have to be proven that medium-altitude UAVs will not cause accidents, and the Federal Aviation Administration will have to work out the air traffic control problems associated with adding drones to private and commercial air traffic.[20]

A major area of focus of the Department of Homeland Security is preventing and responding to a biological weapons attack. The department has launched the BioWatch system, an air-sniffing sensor network designed to detect a biological weapons attack; the system has already been set up in more than thirty major American cities.[21] And the department's Project Bioshield, a $5.6 billion program to build a national stockpile of medicines and vaccines to be used in the event of a biological attack, is also underway.[22] To bring the many programs together and give them strategic direction, the president has signed a classified directive detailing the responsibilities of various agencies in preventing and responding to a biological attack.[23] Beyond this, the Department of Homeland Security has run several major exercises, in conjunction with Canadian officials, simulating WMD terrorist attacks and computer network attacks on critical infrastructures.

To increase security in the air, the Department of Homeland Security has added thousands of armed agents to the federal air marshal program for monitoring commercial flights. From only 30 agents before 11 September 2001, the program has ballooned to over 5,000 armed personnel.[24] The department is also actively exploring the feasibility of outfitting commercial airliners with the type of electronic devices used by some military aircraft to protect them from missiles fired by terrorists on the ground.[25] Despite a huge investment in aviation security, however, there remain many concerns. A report by the DHS and the FBI has assessed that America remains vulnerable to terrorists intent on hijacking non-commercial airplanes and helicopters because these aircraft are subject to less scrutiny than commercial airliners.[26]

One of the most ambitious programs undertaken by the Department of Homeland Security is the United States Visitor and Immigration Status Indicator Technology, or VISIT program, which it launched at more than a dozen major US ports, over a hundred US airports, and about fifty US-Mexico border crossings in 2004. Using a combination of digital photographs, fingerprint scans, and biometrics to trace the unique physical traits of individuals, US-VISIT enables authorities to track visitors to the United States and determine which are still in the country and which have left. The program originated in the Immigration Reform Act of 1996, which was approved by Congress in 2000, but because many of the 9/11 hijackers carried expired visas, it was accelerated after the attacks and specific deadlines were included in the USA Patriot Act of October 2001.[27] Among other stipulations, the act obliges the United States to track entries and exits of individuals from certain countries. The US-VISIT program was originally limited to visitors who required a visa to enter the United States, but it was later expanded to encompass all those permitted to visit the United States for up to ninety days without a visa – including citizens of some of America's closest allies, like Britain and Australia. Given the unique relationship between Canada and the United States and the vast daily transborder flow of people and commerce, Canadian citizens are the only ones in the world (other than American citizens) who are not subject to the program.

Although us-visit is primarily designed to determine which visitors to the United States have overstayed their visas, it is also meant to enable authorities to determine whether an individual should be prohibited from entering the United States in the first place. Here the logic is more problematic, because today the last terrorist act of many terrorists is also their first. The primary threat does not come from known terrorists, but rather from recruits who are groomed for suicide bombing. Clearly, determining the unique physical traits of these individuals will not help to identify threats to US security.

Even once the Department of Homeland Security is fully established, the homeland security mission will still involve other departments. The FBI within the Department of Justice will remain the law enforcement agency that takes the lead in preventing terrorist attacks, and the CIA will continue to gather and analyze overseas intelligence. The Pentagon will continue to be prepared to play a crucial support role in the event of a catastrophic terrorist incident, and the Department of Transportation will continue to be responsible for highway and rail safety and air traffic control. Other departments will also maintain their roles in homeland security.

National Strategy for Homeland Security

How US federal departments will relate to the Department of Homeland Security as they carry out the homeland security mission is tackled in the *National Strategy for Homeland Security*, issued by the White House Office of Homeland Security in July 2002. The strategy encompasses the Department of Homeland Security, but it is much broader in that it also provides direction for other agencies that have a role in homeland security. It organizes homeland security into six critical mission areas – intelligence and warning, border and transportation security, domestic counterterrorism, protection of critical infrastructure and key assets, defence against catastrophic threats, and emergency preparedness and response – and it outlines a number of initiatives in each of these areas. Many of them fall under the purview of the Department of Homeland Security, such as undertaking a container security initiative, creating "smart borders," and establishing an information analysis and infrastructure protection division. But other initiatives go well beyond the department.

In the areas of intelligence and counterterrorism the strategy identifies the need to enhance the analytic capabilities of the FBI and to undertake a complete restructuring of the agency to emphasize the prevention of terrorist attacks. It also states that while law enforcement agencies will continue to investigate and prosecute criminal activity, they should now prioritize preventing and interdicting terrorist activity within the United States. Although the United States has numerous intelligence agencies, no one agency is primarily responsible for domestic intelligence-gathering, as are the Canadian Security Intelligence Service and Britain's MI5. Rather, domestic intelligence-gathering has always been an add-on responsibility of the FBI, and most FBI agents are imbued with a culture that puts being a law enforcement agent first. The result has been that the US intelligence community has historically had little knowledge of domestic vulnerabilities or potential domestic targets.[28] A key weakness behind the intelligence failures of 9/11 is seen by many to be that fact that the FBI is responsible for both law enforcement and domestic intelligence-gathering.

The focus on the prevention of terrorist attacks has already resulted in some fundamental changes at the FBI. The bureau no longer separates criminal and intelligence cases; all cases are now handled jointly, allowing greater access to information on terrorist suspects.[29] In addition, the FBI has moved a substantial amount of its resources and manpower from traditional criminal investigative areas, like organized crime and drugs, to counterterrorism activities.[30] These changes, while significant, still fall short of the complete restructuring of the FBI called for in the *National Strategy*. Substantial differences between the relatively short-term measures necessary to arrest people involved in criminal activity and longer-term measures designed to infiltrate terrorist groups have resulted in calls for a new domestic intelligence service that would reside within the FBI but would be managed by the DCI.[31] At least one study has shown that while having separate security intelligence and law enforcement functions does not prevent problems with operational effectiveness, information-sharing, and accountability, it does create a "culture of prevention" with respect to terrorism, allowing for the disruption of terrorist cells.[32] Nonetheless, the 9/11 Commission rejected the creation of a domestic intelligence agency, citing concerns about possible abuses of civil liberties and the drawbacks of diverting counterterrorism efforts while the threat remains high.[33]

In the area of emergency preparedness and response, the *National Strategy for Homeland Security* identifies planning for military support to civil authorities as a major initiative. It is here that America's Northern Command, created in October 2002, fits into the overall national strategy. The strategy tasks Northern Command with homeland defence and with assisting civil authorities in accordance with US laws. This might include providing technical support and assistance to law enforcement officials, assisting in the restoration of law and order, loaning specialized equipment, or assisting in consequence management (Northern Command is discussed in chapter 5).

The strategy also incorporates the Patriot Act, which is highlighted in the document as helping the intelligence and law enforcement agencies to share information. But in fact the act goes well beyond this. It includes an expanded federal ability to conduct electronic surveillance and execute nationwide search warrants, and it allows for roving wiretaps for listening in on conversations, wide latitude in screening computers (including e-mail messages and e-mail address books), and FBI access to private records. It also allows for immigrants suspected of supporting terrorism to be detained for up to a week without being legally charged with a crime or immigration violation and for the deportation of foreigners who raise money for terrorist groups.

Since the release of the *National Strategy for Homeland Security*, not only has the Department of Homeland Security been created, but also a number of additional subordinate strategies have been released to further detail roles and responsibilities. The *National Strategy to Secure Cyberspace*, released in February 2003, pertains to the responsibility for protecting critical infrastructure and key assets. So, too, does the *National Strategy for the Physical Protection of Critical Infrastructures and Key Assets*, released by the White House the same month. Both the *National Strategy to Combat Weapons of Mass Destruction*, released in December 2003, and the largely classified directive on how the United States should defend itself against biological attacks, released in April 2004, respond to the missions of emergency preparedness and defending against catastrophic terrorism.

HOMELAND SECURITY IN CANADA

Public Safety and Emergency Preparedness Canada

In the aftermath of 9/11 Canada's federal government did not make any immediate organizational-structure changes pertaining to homeland security comparable to the creation of the Department of Homeland Security in the United States. Rather, the government created a special Cabinet committee on public safety and anti-terrorism. Led by former deputy prime minister John Manley, the committee was charged with reviewing policies, legislation, regulations, and programs throughout the government to strengthen Canada's ability to fight terrorism. Manley was Canada's primary contact with Tom Ridge, the first director of the Office of Homeland Security and then the first secretary of the Department of Homeland Security.

When Paul Martin became prime minister, in December 2003, his government announced the creation of the Public Safety and Emergency Preparedness Canada (PSEPC), with Anne McLellan as minister. PSEPC integrates the former Office of Critical Infrastructure Protection and Emergency Preparedness (OCIPEP) and encompasses six agencies, among them those of the former Department of the Solicitor General – including CSIS and the RCMP – and the newly created Canada Border Services Agency (CBSA).

The genesis of the Office of Critical Infrastructure Protection was partly the preparations relating to the so-called Y2K problem – the potential impact of the turn of the century on the computer networks that control the vast majority of contemporary society's critical infrastructures. A parallel concern, based on threat assessments and growing vulnerabilities, was the possibility of a physical or computer network attack on Canada's critical infrastructures. After millennium celebrations came and went without notable failures or interruptions, the prospect of an asymmetric attack on Canada's critical infrastructures moved to centre stage. In February 2001 the government formally created OCIPEP. The new office absorbed the old Emergency Preparedness Canada (EPC), which was roughly equivalent to America's FEMA. Like EPC before it, the office was established as a part of the Department of National Defence, despite having responsibilities that cut across several government departments.

Although OCIPEP has now been integrated into to PSEPC, the original mandate remains in place. The Critical Infrastructure Protection and Emergency Preparedness component of PSEPC is charged with two key missions. First, "to provide national leadership in a new, modern and comprehensive approach to protecting Canada's critical infrastructure," including both its physical and cyber dimensions.[34] PSEPC defines "critical infrastructures" as those physical and information technology facilities, networks, services, and assets that, if disrupted or destroyed, would have a serious impact on the health, safety, security, or economic well-being of Canadians or the effective functioning of Canada's governments. It lists ten sectors that make up Canada's national critical infrastructure: energy and utilities, communications and information technology, finance, health care, food, water, transportation, safety (such as the safety of hazardous materials), government services, and manufacturing. The second mission is to act as the government's primary agent for ensuring national civil emergency preparedness for all types of emergencies, among them natural disasters and those involving weapons of mass destruction.

All of the functions of the former Department of the Solicitor General have also been transferred to PSEPC, including the RCMP and CSIS. Previously, the solicitor general was responsible for protecting Canadians and helping to maintain a peaceful and safe society. The solicitor general was the lead minister for counterterrorism and for coordinating the response to terrorist incidents within the country, including WMD terrorism and physical attacks on critical infrastructures. Under the Security Offences Act, the RCMP has primary investigative responsibility for offences related to terrorism. In the event of a terrorist incident the RCMP would head up the crisis response and law enforcement aspects, while the Emergency Preparedness component of PSEPC would coordinate the consequence management efforts. This division of responsibilities is similar to that between the FBI and FEMA in the United States.

A key component of Canada's security and intelligence community is the Canadian Security Intelligence Service. Created in
1984, CSIS is mandated to collect security intelligence and to provide it to departments of the Government of Canada, provincial
governments, and foreign governments, as required. "Security
intelligence" is intelligence pertaining to threats to the security of
Canada. These threats, in turn, are defined in the CSIS Act as
espionage or sabotage against Canada or Canadian interests; for-
eign-influenced activities within, or relating to, Canada that are
detrimental to its interests; activities within, or relating to, Canada
in support of serious violence against people or property to achieve
a political, religious, or ideological objective within Canada or a
foreign state; and activities directed towards violently overthrow-
ing the Canadian government, like espionage, sabotage, foreign-
influenced activities, or politically motivated violence. CSIS can
collect information related to these threats both in Canada and
abroad. Security intelligence can be distinguished from foreign
intelligence, which is broader in scope. "Foreign intelligence" refers
to information on the capabilities, activities, or intentions of foreign
countries, organizations, or individuals and is required to serve a
country's national (not just security) interests, including economic,
political, military, technological, or environmental objectives.[35]

CSIS has no police powers. Historically, the domestic intelligence-
gathering function was carried out by the security service of the
RCMP, much as domestic intelligence-gathering is a component of
the hitherto primarily law-enforcement-focused FBI. But Canadian
officials ultimately recognized that intelligence-gathering and law
enforcement can be incompatible. As a result, with the creation of
CSIS, the two functions were separated. Canada's decision to separate domestic intelligence-gathering from domestic law enforcement was a sensible one: as noted earlier, prior to the release
of the 9/11 Commission Report, much of the post-9/11 failure-of-
intelligence debate south of the border centred on whether the
FBI's security-intelligence-gathering function should be separated
out and placed in a newly created agency.

In Canada there is growing criticism that the country has only
a limited foreign-intelligence-gathering capability. Unlike many
members of NATO, as well as countries such as Australia and
Sweden, Canada has never had its own foreign intelligence service. Canada gathers its foreign intelligence primarily through the

Communications Security Establishment (CSE). Created in the closing days of World War II, CSE is part of a network of agencies in the United States, Britain, Australia, and New Zealand – known as the UKUSA alliance – that emerged from a successful wartime collaboration to collect signals intelligence, or SIGINT.[36] Valued for its geography, Canada was assigned SIGINT responsibilities for the northern latitudes and polar regions. To this end, it established giant antennas at CFS Alert in Nunavut, CFS Masset in British Columbia, CFB Gander in Newfoundland, and CFS Leitrim south of Ottawa to listen in on the Soviet Union (in the north), maritime transmissions (on the coasts), and diplomatic traffic (out of Ottawa).

Today, CSE has a three-fold mandate: to acquire and distribute foreign signals intelligence; to help protect Canada's electronic information infrastructures; and to assist federal law enforcement and security agencies (the RCMP and CSIS). Much of the mandate centres on satellite communications interception, although its older systems remain in place. The rapid expansion of satellite-based telecommunications in the 1970s prompted the UKUSA network to build satellite communications interception stations in strategic locations for global coverage, one of which is at CFS Leitrim. Extensive refinements to satellite interception technologies in the following two decades led to the creation of a tightly networked interception and processing system, known as Echelon. By employing the Echelon "dictionary," CSE and its partner agencies, notably America's National Security Agency, scan billions of satellite-intercepted conversations, faxes, and e-mails every day for key words that could indicate a security threat. Previously, for reasons related to civil liberties, CSE was limited to intercepting communications between two foreign countries. Canada's Anti-terrorism Act of December 2001 expanded CSE's mandate to include communications between Canada and at least one other country.

Using its electronic eavesdropping techniques, CSE can gather foreign intelligence on individuals, groups, and states. But in the post-9/11 era this has become less salient than human intelligence efforts, because terrorist organizations – Canada's primary security threat – are far less vulnerable than states are to SIGINT interception. Although SIGINT is still very important, increased human intelligence is necessary to identify, penetrate, monitor, and counter the terrorist threat and to gain accurate information on things like the proliferation of weapons of mass destruction and illegal immigration. csis does have liaison offices in some countries, and these are involved in the exchange of security intelligence information concerning threats to the security of Canada. In addition, in recent years csis agents have begun conducting covert operations in foreign countries to gather information about threats to national security.[37] But Canada's foreign-intelligence-gathering capability for human intelligence is still limited, and the country remains heavily dependent on its allies, especially Britain and the United States, for this information.

In the post-9/11 era Canada needs an expanded independent capability to gather human intelligence abroad pertaining to security threats at home. The nature of the international security environment, in which distant events can directly impact Canada, is such that "the centre of gravity of threats to the security of Canada has shifted."[38] Today the physical safety of Canadians at home is more directly linked to circumstances abroad than it has been since the Fenian raids of the mid-1800s. The result is that gathering security intelligence must necessarily start on foreign territory.

Relying on an increased amount of human intelligence from its allies is not a viable option for Canada. The country has relatively small tradable intelligence assets compared to its most important allies, and those allies could be hesitant to provide additional non-reciprocated intelligence.[39] More importantly, Canada needs an independent capability to gather information on threats to domestic security so that it can make its own judgments, interpretations, and threat assessments. However reliable, intelligence from another country will inevitably reflect that country's policy concerns. Moreover, Canada needs to be able to pursue intelligence efforts that are specific to its national interests. In Afghanistan, for example, Canadian troops are engaged in a sometimes perilous mission without an overseas intelligence capability dedicated to protecting them.

Whether an independent capability to gather human intelligence abroad pertaining to security threats to Canada would best be accomplished through the expansion of csis or the creation of a separate agency is an open question. This capability would seem to fall within the third component of csis's mandate – collecting security intelligence pertaining to activities within, or relating to, Canada in support of serious violence against people or property to achieve a political, religious, or ideological objective within Canada or a foreign state. Furthermore, to create a foreign intelligence agency may be to create distinctions between threats at home and threats abroad that are no longer relevant in a globalized world. But, at the same time, for an intelligence agency to divide itself between domestic and foreign operations could be too delicate a balancing act, culturally and legally. Back in 1981 the MacDonald Commission on the RCMP security services (which led to the creation of CSIS) argued that responsibility for security intelligence and foreign intelligence should not be shouldered by a single agency. While a security agency must adhere to the rule of law, a foreign intelligence agency requires a greater degree of flexibility.[40]

CSIS, the RCMP, and Critical Infrastructure Protection and Emergency Preparedness form the core of the new Department of Public Security and Emergency Preparedness. In addition, PSEPC includes the Canada Border Services Agency. Created in December 2003, CBSA is charged with facilitating and managing the movement of goods and people into Canada by administering and enforcing numerous domestic laws and international agreements related to this movement, most notably the Canada-US Smart Border Declaration. CBSA integrates the intelligence interdiction and enforcement program from Citizenship and Immigration Canada, the port of entry program from the Canadian Food Inspection Agency, and the customs program from the Canada Customs and Revenue Agency (renamed the Canada Revenue Agency). The latter move puts customs officers more in line with their American counterparts. In addition to their previous role in collecting cross-border shopping fees, customs officers now perform a public security role, and so they have been issued bulletproof vests and given the authority to arrest and detain people for violations of the Criminal Code of Canada.[41]

The minister of public safety and emergency preparedness also chairs a powerful Cabinet committee on security, public health, and emergencies. Created in December 2003, the committee is charged with managing national security and intelligence issues and activities and coordinating government-wide responses to all emergencies. A future SARS scenario might involve, for example, PSEPC, Health Canada, and Transportation Canada. The committee is to be the centre of political leadership during a crisis, whether the emergency involves public health, a natural disaster, or a threat to national security. It essentially replaces the public safety and anti-terrorism Cabinet committee headed by John Manley, but rather than being ad hoc it is a permanent Cabinet committee and meets on a regular basis.

Although PSEPC can be roughly equated to the Department of Homeland Security, there are some important differences. Most notably, unlike the Department of Homeland Security, PSEPC has no jurisdiction over citizenship and immigration; the reason for this is that the Canadian government wanted to avoid linking threats to national security to foreign-born residents.[42] Another significant difference between PSEPC and the Department of Homeland Security is that in Canada CSIS has become part of PSEPC, while in the United States the CIA and FBI remain outside DHS. Anecdotal evidence suggests that having CSIS and the CBSA in the same organization has facilitated information-sharing between Canadian agencies.[43] Finally, in contrast to the US situation, in Canada the Coast Guard has not been transferred to the central homeland department. In 1995 the Canadian Coast Guard was moved from the Department of Transport to the Department of Fisheries and Oceans. In the wake of 9/11 there has been substantial debate about whether the Coast Guard should now be transferred back to the Department of Transport or granted independent agency status reporting to Parliament and given a new enforcement role more in line with contemporary homeland defence requirements (see chapter 5). Minister McLellan has also suggested that PSEPC could eventually become responsible for the Coast Guard.[44]

The Anti-terrorism Plan

During the Chrétien era Canada did not develop a formal comprehensive plan akin to America's national homeland security strategy. It did, however, implement an anti-terrorism plan with five key objectives: preventing terrorists from arriving in Canada; protecting Canadians from terrorist acts; legislating tools to identify, prosecute, convict, and punish terrorists; keeping the Canada-US border secure and open to legitimate trade; and working with the international community to bring terrorists to justice.

Prime Minister Jean Chrétien's government undertook a wide range of measures in support of these objectives. It expanded its network of immigration control officers at airports around the world to identify and stop terrorists before they could board a plane to Canada. It also introduced a fraud-resistant permanent resident card for all immigrants and permanent residents. With a view to protecting Canadians from terrorist acts, in its security budget of December 2001 the government allocated several billion dollars to increasing intelligence capabilities, improving critical infrastructure protection, enhancing border security, and improving immigrant and refugee claimant screening. In addition, it created the Canadian Air Transport Authority to improve airport screening and to place armed undercover police officers on Canadian aircraft and in airports.

The key new legislative tool to identify, prosecute, convict, and punish terrorists under the anti-terrorism plan is Bill C-36, the Anti-terrorism Act. Passed by Parliament in December 2001, the act granted Canadian law enforcement agencies expanded wiretap powers and the authority to detain anyone for up to seventy-two hours without a warrant on suspicion of terrorism. The government also introduced legislation for a new public safety act that would increase the government's ability to prevent terrorist attacks.[45] Ultimately passed in 2004, the Public Safety Act allows for the collection of air-traveller information, establishes tighter controls over explosives and hazardous materials, increases funding to port security, and enhances the ability of the government to provide a secure environment for air travel.[46] In 2002 the government enacted the Immigration and Refugee Protection Act, which makes it easier for the government to deport individuals deemed a security threat, denies these individuals access to Canada's refugee determination process, and imposes harsher penalties on people-smuggling. And since 9/11 Canada's Financial Transactions and Reports Analysis Centre (FINTRAC) has frozen the assets of more than 400 individuals or organizations associated with terrorism.

In the latter area, halting terrorist financing, it seems apparent that more work needs to be done. Although the Canadian government has made it illegal to raise money for terrorism, experts argue that the response to the problem of terrorist financing has been modest in Canada and elsewhere. No charges have been laid in Canada, and some groups known to have raised large amounts for terrorist activity have yet to be outlawed.[47] In 2004 FINTRAC uncovered more than three times the amount of suspected terrorist financing than in 2003, a reflection of Al Qaeda's increased reliance on financing in Canada and elsewhere as Osama bin Laden's resources have become constrained.[48]

To keep the Canada-US border secure and open to legitimate trade, in December 2001 John Manley and Tom Ridge signed the Canada-US Smart Border Declaration. The objective of this agreement is to increase border security while facilitating the flow of legitimate traffic. To this end, it was accompanied by a thirty-point action plan (now expanded to thirty-two points) that includes a wide range of activities pertaining to the land, air, and maritime environments.

One of the most notable Smart Border initiatives at the Canada-US land border is NEXUS, a clearance system that uses high-tech cards to allow frequent travellers between the two countries – especially business travellers – to cross the border more quickly. Under NEXUS dedicated fast lanes have been established at all major border crossings for pre-approved low-risk travellers. Another initiative is Free and Secure Trade (FAST), a joint Canada-US program for low-risk companies that expedites low-risk shipments across the border in either direction by pre-clearing commercial trucks. This program, too, is in place at all major Canada-US border crossings. Aside from smart cards, Canada and the US are using a wide range of advanced technologies to promote the secure and efficient passage of vehicles across the land border. The Vehicle and Cargo Inspection System (VACIS) uses gamma rays to search trucks and passenger vehicles for explosives, contraband, and people (being smuggled). Radiation detectors mounted on specially equipped trucks at land borders scan trucks and cars for radiation emissions and so-called dirty bombs, and a state of the art video-surveillance system has also been put in place.[49]

Part of the Smart Border Action Plan is to expand the existing Integrated Border Enforcement Teams (IBETS), established as a pilot project in 1996. IBETS are joint Canada-US multi-agency law enforcement teams that target cross-border terrorism and criminal activity. They are made up of Canadian and American police, customs, and immigration officials who work with local, state, and provincial law enforcement agencies to identify, investigate, and interdict organizations and people who pose a threat to national security, such as terrorists or those engaged in organized crime. Under the Smart Border plan, more than twenty IBET teams have been established in fifteen geographic regions along the Canada-US border. In Canada they are supplemented by Integrated National

Security Enforcement Teams (INSETS) located in Vancouver, Toronto, Montreal, and Ottawa. Made up of representatives of federal law enforcement and intelligence agencies, as well as representatives of US law enforcement agencies on a case-by-case basis, INSETS focus exclusively on investigating and exposing terrorist threats.[50]

The Smart Border Action Plan extends beyond land ports of entry to include airports and marine ports. A NEXUS air program has been piloted at selected international airports – including, most recently, Vancouver. In addition, Canada and the United States have agreed to co-locate customs and immigration officers in joint passenger analysis units at major international airports to identify high-risk travellers. At Ottawa International Airport the government is also piloting "dirty bomb" detectors that would warn of radioactive materials in passenger, baggage, or cargo systems. These moves are likely to go some way towards allaying concerns about security in Canadian airports, but there is also a need to increase scrutiny of those who work at airports. A 2004 auditor general's report estimated that as many as 4,500 individuals with access to restricted areas of Canada's airports could have criminal associations that warrant further investigation and possibly the withdrawal of their security clearances.[51]

In the marine environment Canadian and American customs agencies have established joint teams of officials at five ports – Vancouver, Montreal, Halifax, Newark, and Seattle-Tacoma – to examine cargo containers that have been identified electronically in transit as potentially posing a risk. In addition, VACIS gamma ray scanners are being used at Canadian and American ports to look for weapons or contraband inside shipping containers. This has allowed the percentage of cargo containers inspected at Canadian ports to increase from 3 per cent to 8 per cent within a fairly short period.[52] While the increase is significant, the screening process is hardly exhaustive – some experts estimate that it is necessary to inspect 15 to 20 per cent of all cargo containers to have a robust screening process.[53] As is the case with respect to Canada's airports, part of the marine security concern arises from activities at the ports themselves; there is evidence of organized crime and a general lack of policing.[54] Canada's implementation, in 2004, of new international security standards introduced by the International Maritime Organization – including restrictions on unauthorized weapons and limited access to ships and docks – could help improve this situation.

The existence of vast and almost completely unguarded water-ways in the Great Lakes region makes the smuggling of people and drugs across the Canada-US marine border here relatively easy. Currently, Canada has no organization dedicated to the policing and surveillance of the Great Lakes and the St Lawrence Seaway; the RCMP's capacity to interdict on the Great Lakes is "almost non-existent."[55] Increasing security in the Great Lakes region is one of the Bush administration's top priorities, and the United States is likely to press for initiatives in this area as part of any Smart Border II agreement. These could build on the Great Lakes-St Lawrence Seaway Cross-Border Task Force, created soon after 9/11 to target the illicit traffic of people across the maritime part of the Canada-US border and involving numerous Canadian and American military and civilian agencies.[56] To date, Canada has limited its initiatives to increasing security at access points to the Great Lakes, notably the locks on the St Lawrence Seaway.[57]

All of the Smart Border initiatives are likely to be pushed for-ward in the context of the Security and Prosperity Partnership of North America, the framework document for which was signed by the leaders of Canada, Mexico, and the United States in March 2005. The document sets out a broadly defined security agenda (as well as a prosperity agenda) that calls for a common approach to addressing external threats to North America and preventing and responding to threats within North America. More detailed work agendas within these broad goals are to be established and implemented over the coming months and years.[58]

The final component of the anti-terrorism plan is to work with the international community to combat terrorism. Operation Apollo was Canada's military contribution to the international campaign against terrorism from October 2001 to October 2003. At its height, Op Apollo, established in support of America's Operation Enduring Freedom, involved six Canadian warships and 1,500 naval personnel. From January to July 2002 it also included a 750-person battle group deployed at the airport in Kandahar, Afghanistan. In addition, under Operation Athena, Canada con-tributed more than 2,000 personnel to the international security assistance force in Kabul in 2003–04, including a battalion group and a brigade headquarters. Canada's ongoing commitment of more than 900 troops to Afghanistan is likely to increase again in the future.[59]

Border Perceptions

The Smart Border accord and the legislative components of the anti-terrorism plan go to the core of Canadian economic security interests. The United States is by far Canada's largest trading partner, with more than 80 per cent of Canadian exports,[60] representing about 40 per cent of its gross domestic product, going to the United States. Although roughly 25 per cent of America's exports go to Canada, this represents just 2 per cent of its gross domestic product. Canada's much higher percentage means that a border closure is felt far more acutely in Canada than in the United States.

The magnitude of Canada's trade dependence on the United States is such that Canada's access to the American market is more than an economic issue. If one returns to the notion that a threat to national security is something that threatens drastically, and over a relatively brief span of time, to degrade values – including economic values – that Canadians hold essential to their way of life, then it is clear that Canada's access to the US market is also a security issue. Canada has been aware for decades that its economic dependence on the United States is growing, but this reality became glaring in the hours and days after the terrorist attacks, when cross-border traffic came almost to a standstill. Not surprisingly, former CSIS director Ward Elcock has said that while the prospect of a terrorist bomb going off in a major Canadian centre is one of his biggest worries, an equal if not greater worry is the prospect of a terrorist bomb staged from Canada going off in a major US centre.[61]

One of the key reasons the border was all but closed was the perception that Canada has leaky borders and therefore poses a security threat to the United States. None of the nineteen hijackers involved in the 11 September 2001 attacks entered the United States through Canada, but well before the attacks Canada had gained a reputation in the United States as a terrorist haven. This was largely because of the case of Ahmed Ressam, an Algerian who was arrested in December 1999 by an alert US customs agent as he tried to enter the United States, apparently on his way to blow up the Los Angeles airport during New Year's celebrations. Ressam had twice been refused refugee status, yet he continued to live in Montreal, and he carried a (phony) Canadian passport.

Since that time, the auditor general has revealed that in the six years prior to 2003, the Canadian Immigration and Refugee Board lost track of some 36,000 failed refugee claimants who, like Ressam, had been ordered deported.[62] Other reports cited lower figures of between 20,000 and 25,000.[63] Although it is likely that the vast majority of these cases do not represent a security risk – and indeed many may have left the country – in today's security climate it is plausible that at least some of these missing deportees could pose a threat.

The Ressam incident clearly highlighted the necessity for Canada to tighten its immigration, customs, and security laws. Enhancing the scrutiny of immigrant and refugee claimants has been an area of significant focus for Canada, and the Immigration and Refugee Protection Act has allowed the government to strengthen its management of immigrants and refugees. Canada now, for example, detains suspicious refugee applicants, no longer allowing them to go free until their hearings, and their detention period could last for up to two years. The United States, too, has strengthened its laws concerning immigrants and refugees, and, through its US-VISIT program, it has tightened up the screening and monitoring of visitors and other temporary entrants. This is a step that Canada has so far declined to take. As a result, Canada has no means of knowing if its visitors, whether they are tourists, students, or temporary workers, comply with the terms of their visas, attend the schools in which they are enrolled, work with their designated employers, or leave when their visas expire.[64] Potential wrongdoers could see this as a more attractive area for exploitation than it was in the past because of the tighter rules for immigration and refugee claimants.

Much of the perception surrounding Canada's lax borders is just that – perception. The only concrete instance of a terrorist getting past the Canadian border to the United States is the Ressam case. Although it is true that Canada has lost track of roughly 25,000 refugee claimants, there are millions of unaccounted-for persons in the United States. Of the estimated seven or eight million unauthorized people living in America, the vast majority are from Mexico, and to a lesser extent other Central American countries, while less than 1 per cent have come from Canada.[65] By contrast, more than 50 per cent of people seeking refugee status in Canada every year come from the United States.[66] In 2002 this figure was over 13,000.[67] Moreover, about 80 per cent of the refugees entering Canada from high-risk countries come through the US.[68]

As part of the Smart Border Action Plan, Canada and the United States negotiated and signed the Safe Third Country Agreement in 2002. Once implemented, it will significantly reduce the number of claimants arriving at Canadian borders. According to the terms of the agreement, refugees would have to make their claims in the first of the two countries they enter.[69] Thus, claimants trying to enter Canada through the United States would be turned back and told to make their claims in the United States (and vice versa). To date the United States has been slow to implement the agreement. Progress in this area will clearly involve convincing the United States to implement the accord it has signed – something the minister of public safety and emergency preparedness is pursuing with her American counterpart. But Canada and the United States should also consider examining why it is – other than for reasons of family reunification – that asylum shoppers choose to shop in Canada. Although Canadian and US refugee systems are similar in many ways, they also have some important differences, including the way they define "refugee." As a result, some refugees who would be accepted by Canada would be refused by the United States. As long as there are significant distinctions between the two systems, those seeking to enter Canada will employ increasingly desperate methods, as evidenced by the case of the 130 Chinese immigrants who were smuggled to a remote section of Canada's western coast aboard a Korean ship in August 1999. Without a greater harmonization of definitions, the Safe Third Country Agreement could merely serve to increase claimants' vulnerability to smugglers. Not surprising, a high-level task force on the future of North America has recommended the harmonization of asylum regulations.[70]

National Security Policy

Under Prime Minister Paul Martin, the federal government has sought to put Canada's approach to national security on a more formal footing by releasing Canada's first-ever national security policy. *Securing an Open Society: Canada's National Security Policy* highlights three core national security interests: protecting Canada and Canadians at home and abroad, ensuring that Canada is not a base for threats to our allies, and contributing to international security. Although the policy's purported scope is comprehensive, in fact the vast majority of its initiatives pertain to the first two interests, leaving the third to be filled by Canada's International Policy Statement of April 2005. Moreover, much of the National Security Policy includes a restatement of steps that had already been taken by the Canadian government in the years since 9/11. Nonetheless, the policy is useful because it put existing activities into an overall framework, and in doing so it identified important gaps in Canada's security measures.

One of the gaps is the fact Canada had no central organization charged with fusing intelligence from all members of the security and intelligence community. Comprised of those federal agencies and departments that provide the Government of Canada with intelligence information on specific threats to Canadian safety and security, the community includes CSIS, the RCMP, the CSE, the Department of National Defence, the Department of Foreign Affairs, the Privy Council Office, the PSEPC, Transport Canada, and the CBSA. Coordination of the various agencies and departments has historically been the responsibility of the Privy Council Office, a task that was made relatively simple by the predictable adversarial dynamics of Cold War intelligence. But the traditional coordinating mechanism of periodic consultative meetings, which remained in place throughout the 1990s, proved unsuited to the increased intelligence demands of the post-9/11 era. Therefore, *Securing an Open Society: Canada's National Security Policy* announced the creation of the Integrated Threat Assessment Centre, which brings together on an ongoing basis intelligence from all members of the intelligence community and provides this information to those who require it. The centre is housed in CSIS, but it includes representatives of all departments and agencies that are members of the security and intelligence community and works closely with the national security adviser in the Privy Council Office.

The policy also seeks a more integrated approach to emergency preparedness, whether a particular crisis involves a health pandemic like SARS, the terrorist use of weapons of mass destruction, or a natural disaster. A new government operations centre has been created in PSEPC to provide around-the-clock coordination of key players at the federal, provincial, and municipal levels in the event of a national emergency. One key player in many types of emergency would likely be the Canadian Forces, which would support civilian agencies (see chapter 5). Another would be the new Public Health Agency of Canada, created in response to the SARS crisis to develop national strategies for managing infectious diseases. Still another would likely be Health Canada, which is working on bio-security issues with the US Department of Health and Human Services under the Smart Border agreement. The overall objective of the policy is to create an integrated security system that includes integrated threat assessment; protection against, and prevention of, threats; emergency response; and oversight.[71]

Like America's National Strategy for Homeland Security, Canada's national security policy paves the way for additional subordinate strategies, which some officials have argued are long overdue.[72] The government plans to develop a critical infrastructure protection strategy in conjunction with provincial, territorial, and private sector leaders as well as the United States. It also plans to release a national cyber-security strategy designed to reduce Canada's vulnerability to cyber-attacks and cyber-accidents.

More than anything, the national security policy is meant to assure America that Canada's 1938 security pledge still holds: Canada will not allow threats access to the United States via land, sea, or air across Canadian territory.[73] Continued fulfillment of this decades-old commitment is the intention behind the explicit statement that one of Canada's core national security objectives is to ensure that Canada is not a base for threats to its allies. "We refuse to be a weak link or a haven from which terrorists can attack others," argued PSEPC Minister Anne McLellan when the policy was released. "We have a choice in Canada – to be in denial or be prepared."[74] Being prepared involves numerous civilian measures, but it also requires some military-led initiatives. The next chapter examines the second quadrant of security policy responses: military activities at home that are necessary for guaranteeing North American security.

5

Homeland Defence

Homeland defence is part of the broader concept of homeland security. The term "homeland defence" refers to military-led activities aimed at guaranteeing the security of a nation's people or property. Traditionally, these activities have been directed against external threats, and such threats continue to be a major area of focus. But in the post-9/11 era there is also a need for military responses to internal threats, like the hijacking of airplanes in domestic airspace, as well as a greater degree of military support to civilian agencies than there has been historically.

This chapter traces significant developments in homeland defence south and north of the border since 11 September 2001 and looks at joint initiatives between the United States and Canada. Much is going on in both countries, but perhaps the most interesting story concerns the measures they have taken cooperatively. The nature of the threat to North America today demands an integration of Canadian and American defence measures that goes well beyond the framework of Canada-US defence cooperation that existed throughout the Cold War period.

HOMELAND DEFENCE IN THE UNITED STATES

NORTHCOM

One key institutional development in response to the post-9/11 security environment has been the creation of US Northern Command. Since shortly after World War II, the US military has divided the world into several areas of responsibility, each of which is overseen by a joint or unified command that brings together elements of the army, navy, air force, and Marine Corps. The number of commands, as well as their names and specific regional scope, has changed over the years, and the US Unified Command Plan updates the situation on a biennial basis. Today the plan includes nine commands, four of which are functional and five of which are geographic.[1]

The geographic command of Northern Command, or NORTHCOM, was established in October 2002 and is headquartered at Peterson Air Force Base in Colorado Springs. Assigned a region that encompasses the continental United States, Canada, Mexico, and portions of the Caribbean, NORTHCOM has overall responsibility for the homeland defence of the United States and is specifically responsible for the defence of America's land approaches and sea approaches extending out 500 miles. Its mandate also includes collaborating with the Department of Homeland Security on civil support missions, including responding to terrorist attacks, and military coordination with Canada and Mexico. The commander of Northern Command doubles as commander of the North American Aerospace Defence Command, or NORAD, which is the joint Canada-US command responsible for the aerospace defence of North America. In this capacity, the commander of Northern Command is also in charge of all the combat air patrols conducted over American cities (discussed later in this chapter). The arrangement ensures that overall responsibility for the air, land, and sea components of defending the United States resides in one agency. In addition, the commander of Northern Command has been assigned responsibility for America's fledgling ballistic missile defence system for North America.

In addition, the commander of Northern Command/NORAD will potentially be commander of any future ballistic missile defence system for North America.

A joint military command dedicated to the defence of North America is an entirely new element in US defence planning. Previously, US Atlantic Command was responsible for all the forces assigned to defending the continental United States, but its commander was also commander of NATO's Atlantic Command. In the late 1990s Atlantic Command was renamed Joint Forces Command and given the further responsibility of spearheading the US military's force-transformation efforts. Defending the United States was never the exclusive mission of either Atlantic Command or Joint Forces Command. Moreover, neither command had geographic responsibility for Canada (or Mexico); defence relations with Canada were conducted on a bilateral basis by the Pentagon and through NORAD, and on a multilateral basis through NATO. (The only other country never assigned to a command – and with which relations were conducted directly by the Pentagon – was Russia, which is now part of European Command.)

Although US Northern Command plans, organizes, and executes homeland defence and civil support missions, it has few permanent forces. Rather, the command is assigned forces whenever necessary to execute missions as ordered by the president. That said, NORTHCOM has been assigned on a permanent basis the Joint Task Force civil support units that used to be part of Joint Forces Command and that were created in the late 1990s to provide command and control of military forces in support of civil authorities in the event of a WMD attack on US soil.

The Role of the US Military in Homeland Security

US military officials have stressed that in all cases in which NORTHCOM's forces operate inside the United States they will support federal, state, or local civilian agencies.[2] This is important, because one of the issues raised in the *National Strategy for Homeland Security* (see chapter 4) is the role of the military in domestic law enforcement activities. The *Posse Comitatus Act*[3] of 1878 and amplifying Department of Defense regulations dating to 1982 generally bar the use of military personnel in civilian law enforcement activities in the United States, including investigating and arresting individuals.[4] But the 9/11 attacks prompted a debate within the United States as to whether these limits on the role of the military in homeland security should be reassessed. The debate was most vocal among some members of Congress, who pressed at the time for thousands of National Guard members to be deployed along America's borders to stop illegal immigration.[5] Reflecting this sentiment, the *National Strategy for Homeland Security* argues, "The threat of catastrophic terrorism requires a thorough review of the laws permitting the military to act within the United States in order to determine whether domestic preparedness and response efforts would benefit from greater involvement of military personnel and, if so, how."[6]

To date, calls for a military role in domestic law enforcement activities have not been acted upon. In the wake of 9/11 National

Guard units were in fact deployed along the Canadian and Mexican borders, but this was only on an interim basis, for six months, and the troops were not armed. The military is strongly opposed to assuming a law enforcement role; its view is that military personnel are trained to fight wars, not conduct police operations. Moreover, large segments of the civilian population would likely be concerned about the civil liberties implications. Northern Command's official Web page states explicitly that "in understanding the difference between Homeland Security and Homeland Defense, it is important to understand that NORTHCOM is a military organization whose operations within the United States are governed by law, including the *Posse Comitatus Act*."[7] Others, however, make a convincing case that the act itself "is not a significant impediment to DoD participation in law enforcement and homeland security" – rather, it is the DoD regulations surrounding the law that have imposed the restrictions.[8]

Notwithstanding the legal debate, NORTHCOM is looking at how to better provide military support to civil authorities. One option could be to assign a greater homeland security role to the National Guard, which has historically been trained and equipped as a strategic reserve for overseas combat. Well before the 9/11 attacks, the US Commission on National Security/21ST Century urged that "the National Guard be given homeland security as a primary mission, as the US Constitution itself ordains."[9] US military reserve components include the National Guard – made up of the air and army National Guards of each state and normally commanded by the state governor – and the army, navy, air force, Marine Corps, and Coast Guard reserves commanded by the president. If mobilized as federal troops to support domestic missions, National Guard units would be commanded by NORTHCOM. (Notably, the *Posse Comitatus Act* does not apply to the National Guard if it is commanded by the state.)[10] Alternatively, US Northern Command is also considering creating a dedicated homeland defence force consisting of designated reserve units in each of the fifty states, an arrangement that would result in a shorter chain of command for call-out at the federal level.[11]

A Strategy for Homeland Defence and Civil Support

Decisions in these areas are likely to be made in the context of a much broader strategy for homeland defence and civil support being prepared by the Pentagon. Billed as the "first effort to craft a cohesive policy for using the military to protect the United States since the war on terrorism began," the strategy calls for major improvements in the way the military acts to prevent a homeland incident or supports local and state authorities in the aftermath of a disaster.[12] Likely elements of the strategy include: establishing a sensor architecture for homeland defence; ensuring that the military can communicate with first-responders; identifying ways to improve defence intelligence for homeland defence; developing a concept of operations to improve maritime defence; doing the same for cruise missile defence; planning to expand the use of the National Guard for homeland defence and civil support missions; examining requirements for the domestic military use of non-lethal weapons; and looking at the training and readiness requirements of military forces likely to be called on by civilian authorities in the event of a mass-casualty attack on the homeland. Improvements in maritime defence are a particular area of focus, with the navy's littoral combat ship being touted as the ideal platform to defend territorial waters because of its ability to move at high speeds and to operate in shallow waters.[13]

HOMELAND DEFENCE IN CANADA

Like the United States, Canada has never had a joint military command dedicated to the defence of the homeland. "In the past, Canada has structured its military primarily for international operations, while the domestic role has been treated as a secondary consideration," notes the Martin government's international policy statement. "Clearly, this approach will no longer suffice."[14] As a result, the defence component of the document sets out plans to significantly restructure the Canadian Forces for the homeland defence of Canada. With a view to treating Canada as "a single operational area," the government has decided to establish six regional headquarters across the country that integrate land, sea, and air elements.[15] These headquarters will report, in turn, to a single integrated command structure, Canada Command, broadly analogous to America's Northern Command. Canada Command came into force in the summer of 2005, and the first regional headquarters was established in Halifax. The time frame for subsequent headquarters has yet to be determined, but it is likely that

Canada Command will be operational across the country by spring 2006.

When it comes to homeland defence, Canada's military forces are tasked with ensuring the physical security of Canadians and the defence of Canada's sovereignty, in addition to the defence missions of contributing to continental security, international stability, and promoting basic human rights and freedoms abroad.[16] Specific responsibilities in the first two areas include performing surveillance and controlling Canadian approaches and territory; assisting civil authorities in countering terrorist and asymmetric threats, as well as in ensuring critical-infrastructure protection and emergency preparedness; and aid of the civil power in accordance with section 275 of the *National Defence Act*.[17]

Maritime Surveillance and Control

Canada's military capabilities for the surveillance and control of its maritime approaches are quite limited. Its eighteen Aurora long-range patrol aircraft travel about once a week up and down the east and west coasts, and semi-annually over the Arctic. At any given time several of the aircraft are out of service because they are being upgraded with a ground moving target indicator capability to enable them to track movements on land and at sea; they already have a subsurface surveillance capability dating from the Cold War. The navy's twelve maritime coastal defence vessels (MCDV) conduct surveillance missions along the coasts, but since they have no ability to operate in ice-infested waters, they are limited as to how far north they can go. Once they are fully operational Canada's four Victoria-class submarines will be able to conduct surveillance missions off the east and west coasts and in the summer months travel as far north as the Northwest Passage.

Canada's long-range patrol aircraft, coastal patrol vessels, and submarines cannot provide continuous surveillance of Canada's maritime approaches. To fill some of the gaps Canada is turning to advanced technology. The Canadian Forces (CF) is setting up a chain of long-range radar stations, called the High Frequency Surface Wave Radar Network, along the east and west coasts to keep watch on the maritime approaches. The network will involve eight radars, two on the west coast and six on the east, each of which can detect ships or low-flying aircraft up to 200 nautical miles (or 350 kilometres) away as they approach the Gulf of St Lawrence or the Straits of Juan de Fuca.[18] Two sites on the east coast have already been activated, and the plan is for all eight stations to be up and running by 2008.[19] Once in place the radar sites will form a sort of naval version of the North Warning System of NORAD radars.

Looking further ahead, the Department of National Defence (DND) is designing a deep-sea tripwire system using a string of acoustic sensors anchored to the ocean floor. Dubbed the Rapidly Deployable System, it would involve quickly and strategically placing sensors underwater at specific points off the coast where intelligence indicated a smuggler or terrorist threat. The sensors would pick up sounds of approaching surface or underwater vessels and relay this information to shore for further investigation. Experimental sensors will soon be available, but a full system (if funded) would take ten to fifteen years to develop.[20] The CF is also experimenting with robotic aircraft, or unmanned aerial vehicles (UAVs), to determine how such drones can be used to monitor Canada's approaches. "Today, if I want to have a look at something, I have to sail a ship or have to task an Aurora patrol aircraft," points out the commander of Canadian Forces Pacific. "With ... UAV[s] ... you would have the capability to send a vehicle out to localize the area of the contact and even to take a picture."[21] In the summer of 2003 the CF tested unmanned aerial vehicles off Vancouver Island to see how drones could be used to detect smugglers, and the following summer it tested a version of America's Predator unmanned aircraft over Baffin Island to see whether UAVs could be adapted to the extreme conditions of the North. The CF hopes to have an operational UAV capability for Arctic surveillance and perhaps sovereignty and counterterrorism patrols off the coasts by 2008.[22]

Canada is also limited in the control component of maritime surveillance and control. The frigate provides an important Canadian military capability for maritime interdiction missions around North America that are some distance off shore. Maritime helicopters enhance the surveillance and interdiction capabilities of Canada's frigates and destroyers, and so the decision to replace Canada's fleet of aging Sea King maritime helicopters is an important one.[23] Submarines can also be used for interdiction. Canada's ships normally operate as a naval task group – usually involving a destroyer, one or more frigates, and a replenishment vessel – and these task groups are well suited to the maritime surveillance and control of the waters off North America.[24] Closer to shore, however, Canada has very little capability. The navy's coastal defence vessels are armed, but because they were designed for patrolling and mine warfare they are not very fast and are therefore unsuitable for interdiction. Moreover, these vessels are too small to handle the rough seas off some parts of Vancouver Island and the Grand Banks of Newfoundland – yet the frigates are too big, in the sense of being costly.[25] The requirement in the post-9/11 security environment is for a mid-sized naval vessel to carry out armed, non-military tasks in support of other government departments in Canada's territorial waters.

The Coast Guard

Off Canadian shores the RCMP is overstretched. It has only a few boats and limited personnel to carry out enforcement missions along hundreds of miles of coastline. The Coast Guard has the appropriate vessels for interdiction missions within two or three miles of the coast, but neither the security mandate nor the weaponry to intervene in criminal activity. For these reasons, it would be useful to reconsider the Coast Guard's mandate.

In contrast to the American Coast Guard, the Canadian Coast Guard has never been an enforcement or security agency. Transport Canada is the lead department for marine security in Canada; the RCMP conducts police functions along the coasts, assisted, if necessary, by the navy. The Coast Guard can support enforcement agencies by transporting armed officers from the Department of Fisheries, the RCMP, or Citizenship and Immigration Canada to vessels of interest. But the general coastal protection role remains the navy's.[26] This somewhat confusing framework, with its sometimes overlapping agency mandates, has been compared with the US situation in the following terms:

Looking at the mission of national defence for the country and establishing a boundary around the country, that is the sole responsibility of the navy. Whether you draw that line 200 miles off the coast or whatever, the navy takes responsibility and protects the coasts, conducts regular surveillance, monitors the situation, and basically interdicts and does the high seas missions. As you start getting in closer to the country, other players come to the table. Domestic industry, container shipping, vessels that move cargo and so on ... [are] the responsibility of Transport Canada. They look at registering vessels, licensing them, and protecting them. The regulatory component is done by the Canadian Coast Guard. Port protection, control of shipping within the St Lawrence Seaway and so forth fall as a mission to the Department of Transport. Drug traffic on the coasts is a police responsibility. The military has the capacity to deliver interdiction teams to vessels of interest. We do not do the boarding, and we do not do the arrest, but we assist the RCMP in conducting that operation at sea. When you go to the United States, you enter a different domain with different players. Their Coast Guard functions as an interdiction agent within 200 miles. There is a standing agreement in the United States where the navy basically looks out 200 miles and beyond and the Coast Guard looks in 200 miles.[27]

Thus, when it comes to operations off Canada's coasts, a whole host of players are involved on the Canadian side. An exercise in and around the approaches to Esquimalt Harbour and the Straits of Juan de Fuca in 2005, for example, involved the US Coast Guard, the Canadian navy, the Canadian Coast Guard, Transport Canada, the RCMP, and the CBSA.[28] To bring together the intelligence gathered by various government departments about activity off Canada's coasts, the navy is developing maritime security operations centres in Victoria and Halifax. The centers will use advanced technologies to combine information from the agencies and present it in a coordinated fashion, thereby giving a comprehensive picture of what is happening along Canada's coasts. In future the network could be expanded to include monitoring the Great Lakes and the St Lawrence Seaway.[29]

The fact that numerous players are involved in Canada's marine security, combined with the increased imperative in the post-9/11 security environment that these agencies work well together, led to the creation of the Interdepartmental Marine Surveillance Working Group soon after the terrorist attacks. Led by Transport Canada, the group is mandated to coordinate Canada's response to marine security, analyze the marine system for any security gaps, and develop initiatives to address those gaps. The efforts of the working group have already led to the announcement, in 2003, of $170 million over five years to fund a series of initiatives designed to close marine security gaps. They include the Automatic Identification System and Long Range Vessel Identification and Tracking Project, which involves the Department of Fisheries and Oceans, Transport Canada, and the Coast Guard; another such initiative is DND's High Frequency Surface Wave Radar Network (noted earlier).

Some believe that much more is required. The House of Commons Fisheries Committee has argued that the Coast Guard should be returned to the Department of Transport (from Fisheries and Oceans) and given a new mandate as an armed maritime security agency to help protect the country.[30] Similarly, the Standing Senate Committee on National Security and Defence has stated that the Coast Guard should play a constabulary role on Canada's coasts, with national security taking precedence over its other duties.[31] Although the navy could be furnished with speedy, shallow-draft vessels appropriate for navigating ports and bays – and such a project is in the works in the defence services program[32] – this capability would not resolve the difficult political issue of having military forces performing a lead role along Canadian shores. Equipping and training the Coast Guard for a security role close to shore – and in the Great Lakes region – is a sensible long-term solution to the increased policing and interdiction requirements of the post-9/11 security environment. The Coast Guard knows Canada's shoreline best, and assigning it an enforcement role would allow the RCMP to concentrate its resources on land. Such a mission change would demand a significant cultural shift. Nonetheless, it is a necessary transition, one that is consistent with adaptations already made by land-border customs officers, who have made public security – instead of cross-border shopping – their primary area of focus (see chapter 4).

The Arctic

In improving its capabilities in the area of surveillance and control, Canada will have to pay greater attention to the Arctic. There is growing debate over the implications to Canadian sovereignty of global warming and the melting polar ice cap. One expert opinion is that the Northwest Passage will not be ice-free for some decades. Although it will become navigable within the next ten years, it will remain ice-infested and therefore hold little attraction for international shipping lines.[33] Another view is that although future ice conditions are not precisely known, even if the waters are ice-infested the economic incentives will be such that at least some ships will transport goods between Europe, North America's eastern seaboard, and Asia by sailing through the passage.[34] A 2001 report by the US Department of the Navy argues that as a result of global warming, non-ice-strengthened ships will be able to make regular use of the Northwest Passage for at least one month each summer beginning sometime between 2007 and 2012.[35] *Canada's International Policy Statement* foresees commercial traffic through the Arctic as early as 2015.[36]

Although there are diverging opinions as to whether the Northwest Passage will become an international waterway anytime soon, it seems apparent that, at the very least, maritime activity in and around the Northwest Passage will increase over the next decade. At the same time the Arctic is of growing interest because of its resources. A number of circumpolar countries are in the process of mapping the extent of their continental shelves in order to lay claim to any reserves of oil and gas in the ocean floor.[37] As resource development continues across the North, there is also concern that terrorists could see the Arctic as the "soft underbelly of the continent"; already the expanding diamond trade in the Northwest Territories has drawn organized criminal elements.[38]

The combination of these factors means that there is an almost immediate requirement for Canada to increase its ability to conduct surveillance of the Arctic. Under Project Polar Epsilon, scheduled to be operational by 2006 or 2007, the CF is buying time on a commercial satellite system, Radarsat 2, to gain regular and frequent wide-area, space-based surveillance information about Canada's vast Arctic land mass. Polar Epsilon will enable the military not only to monitor the waters and coastline of the Arctic for traditional threats to Canada's security, like weapons and military movements, but also to watch for emergencies and environmental disasters. Canada is also considering acquiring unmanned aerial vehicles for surveillance of the Arctic (noted earlier) and extending the High Frequency Surface Wave Radar Network to include sites that will look at each end of the Northwest Passage.[39] In the longer term Canada will need a capability to conduct maritime patrols. The melting ice cap will increase the stretch of northern waters in which Canada's diesel submarines can operate without restrictions,[40] and the annual number of weeks during which they will be able to do so. Once it enters service, in about 2010, Canada's new joint support ship (see chapter 7) will also have a limited ability to operate in Arctic areas.[41] But none of Canada's present naval vessels can operate in ice-infested waters,[42] and Canada's largest Arctic icebreaker, the Coast Guard's massive *Louis St Laurent*, is almost beyond refurbishing.[43]

The Role of the Canadian Military in Homeland Security

The CF's regular force members play a significant role in providing assistance to civil authorities in countering terrorist and asymmetric threats. For many years they have been trained to deal with weapons of mass destruction in an overseas environment. A nuclear, biological, and chemical weapons school was established at Canadian Forces Base Borden during the Cold War, for example, long before it was ever expected that such expertise would be needed at home. It only makes sense that the military's skills in this area be used in the event of a WMD terrorist attack on North American soil. Therefore, the CF has developed units that can be called out to assist civilian authorities if necessary. The Joint Nuclear, Biological and Chemical Defence Company, which has about one hundred regular force personnel drawn from the army, navy, and air force, has been established at Canadian Forces Base Trenton and is likely to be expanded.[44] Joint Task Force 2, Canada's special operations force based outside Ottawa, is also trained to operate in a WMD-contaminated environment at home and abroad. In the event of a WMD-related terrorist incident in Canada, these units could be called upon to assist the RCMP in responding to the crisis.

In the post-9/11 era there are calls for the CF's military reserves to play an expanded role in homeland security and defence. These calls are tied directly to changes in the international security environment, but they are better understood in the context of the ongoing debate over the role of the army reserves, or militia, that well predates the 11 September attacks. Back in 1995 the Canadian government, recognizing there was a host of problems with the land force reserves – relating to everything from roles and tasks to organization and administration – launched the Special Commission on the Restructuring of the Reserves. The commission put forward numerous recommendations, which were then monitored by the Minister's Monitoring Committee, created in 1997 to track progress in implementing recommendations from a wide range of CF-related reports that had been produced over the previous few years. In 1999 the committee, chaired by the Honourable John Fraser, issued its final report on the full range of studies it was tasked to monitor. Meanwhile, concurrent work in the Department of National Defence Land Force Reserve Restructure Program reached an impasse, and the Minister's Monitoring Committee was tasked to examine the situation. The result was another report, which focused specifically on the land force reserves.[45] The government accepted the report, issued a policy statement on land force reserve restructure in October 2000, and tasked the committee with monitoring the statement's implementation. An interim report was presented to the minister early in 2002 and a final report late in 2003.

The most basic questions surrounding the army reserve concern its role and operational tasks. These questions do not arise as often with the naval and air reserves because the navy and air force have found specific and valid roles for their reserves. Naval reserves crew the maritime coastal defence vessels, while air reserves fly two squadrons of Griffon helicopters and otherwise are integrated into regular air force flights.[46] It has proven more difficult to assign a specific role to the militia. After World War II it was assigned the task of mobilizing in addition to assisting the regular army in the defence of Canada. But as the Cold War took hold mobilization came to be considered a dead issue; there would not be enough time to mobilize during a nuclear war. Prime Minister John Diefenbaker responded to the threat of thermonuclear war by assigning civil defence duties to the militia. The army, despite its bitter resistance, was compelled to retrain its reserve component for "national survival" duties, like rescuing and feeding survivors of nuclear war.[47] Many units lost their heavy weapons and armoured vehicles.

Once NATO adopted a strategy of flexible response, in the 1960s, mobilization for a long war increased in importance and the militia resumed its previous role. Nonetheless, personnel and equipment levels continued to decline over the next several decades. The 1994 *Defence White Paper* identified the primary role of the reserves as the augmentation, sustainment, and support of deployed forces,[48] while the 1995 Special Commission similarly stated the militia "must be organized and trained to provide augmentation for the regulars and to be capable of expansion to meet mobilization needs."[49] The 2000 government statement on land force reserve restructure identified the raison d'être of the militia as providing the framework for expansion and mobilization of forces, augmenting deployed units and individuals on peace support operations, and representing a "footprint" in communities across the country.

Today discussions are underway in which the militia is addressed as something far greater than a footprint. At the political level, former defence minister David Pratt's office touted the military reserves as "the first line of defence" in the event of a terrorist attack on Canadian soil, arguing that the reserves must augment the regular force and be prepared to be called out en masse in support of civilian first-responders in times of national emergency.[50] Similarly, at the military level, the CF's project manager for the Land Force Reserve Restructure Program has recommended adding "a layer of first-responders – citizen soldiers" who can rush to an NBC attack, wherever it may occur.[51] He envisions an expanded role for Canada's militia that would see highly trained security platoons deployed almost immediately to help civilian authorities. This idea is consistent with the view expressed in a Senate committee report that army reserves should be employed across the country as chemical, biological, radiological, and nuclear defence specialists assisting local first-responders.[52] The idea of the reserves providing response units to handle a nuclear, chemical, or biological incident is still under examination. Meanwhile, the CF is already establishing community planning officers in cities across the country to work with police, fire, and ambulance officials in determining the types of incidents that could affect a city – from earthquakes to terrorist attacks – and to draw up plans to deal with such a crisis. The planning officers are to act as the community's point of contact in accessing the resources of the entire Canadian Forces.[53]

Although these new roles will see the army reserves making a greater contribution to homeland defence, decision-makers at the political and military levels insist that the overseas role will remain in place. This marks the major distinction between today's renewed homeland emphasis and the civil defence mandate of the Diefenbaker era. As the Minister's Monitoring Committee's progress report of 2002 pointed out, in the contemporary security environment the three roles of footprint, mobilization, and augmentation are not mutually exclusive.[54] "Given the changing nature of the threat to Canada all army units must be capable of dual use ... of responding to expeditionary [requirements] or domestic threats."[55]

The new thinking on the role of the reserves in Canada reflects a shift that has already taken place among Canada's allies, notably Britain. In its *Strategic Defence Review* (SDR) of 1998 Britain concluded that given the vastly decreased threat of hostilities on British soil, maintaining the territorial army for homeland defence was no longer a relevant defence mission.[56] Four years later, *The Strategic Defence Review: A New Chapter* concluded that there was a greater role for the reserves to play in supporting civil authorities and proposed the creation of a dozen 500-person reaction forces from the volunteer reserves for the purposes of home defence and security.[57]

Aid of the Civil Power

The key distinction between the CF assisting civil authorities and acting in the aid of the civil power is that in the latter scenario the CF temporarily becomes the lead agency because it is beyond the power of the civil authorities to suppress, prevent, or deal with the situation. In the contemporary security environment this is quite a plausible circumstance. A WMD terrorist attack against a civilian population could create a sense of panic greater than the actual effects of the weapons.[58] Alternatively, it could incapacitate first-responders and render them unable to deal with the situation. In either case, the military would need to take control of the situation. That is to say, soon after a WMD terrorist attack the Canadian Forces would likely no longer be *assisting* a civilian lead agency; rather, the CF would *be* the lead agency.

For such a mission the CF's regular forces should be able to deploy on short notice, anywhere in Canada, a reaction force of about 500 regular force personnel to respond to a chemical, biological, radiological, or terrorist attack. This would involve maintaining at high readiness forces trained to operate in a WMD-contaminated environment, as well as Hercules aircraft to transport personnel. Strategic airlift would be necessary to get equipment across the country quickly. Indeed, getting from one end of Canada to another is almost as strategic in terms of distance as getting to places abroad. Canada was forced to rely on US strategic airlift to transport CF military equipment to Manitoba during the 1997 Red River flood. In the event of a major disaster, like an earthquake in British Columbia, Canada would be unable to independently deploy its (Kingston-based) Disaster Assistance Response Team. Beyond this, there would also be the requirement for crowd control and other functions traditionally associated with aid of the civil power. It is likely that additional forces, beyond the roughly 500-person reaction force, would be necessary, and these could be drawn from the reserves. An expanded joint nuclear, biological, and chemical defence company would usefully provide the core of this capability, as would the Special Operations Group – one of three new kinds of joint formation the CF is in the process of establishing for homeland defence and for operations abroad.[59] The others, the Standing Contingency Task Force and several mission-specific task forces, could also respond to domestic crises and emergencies.[60]

HOMELAND DEFENCE –
THE UNITED STATES AND CANADA

Air Surveillance and Control

The primary means through which Canada conducts surveillance and control of its air approaches is NORAD. Established in 1957, NORAD is a binational, Canada-US command for the air defence of North America headquartered in Colorado Springs. Over the years NORAD's mission has evolved with the changing threat environment. It first assumed air defence against bombers, then it took on aerospace warning of ballistic missiles, and finally it added the surveillance and monitoring of aircraft suspected of illegal drug trafficking. Throughout this period, and even with the new types of missions of the post–Cold War era, one feature of NORAD remained consistent: it always looked outward to address threats approaching the continent.

The most dramatic change in NORAD's mission post-9/11 is that it has broadened its focus from looking exclusively outward to looking both outward and inward at potential airborne threats. NORAD is still responsible for detecting, identifying, and, if necessary, intercepting potentially threatening air traffic entering North American airspace, but it has also adjusted to a new mission of handling threats arising from within the continent. A good example of resulting changes in NORAD's operating procedures is that today the NORAD operations centre listens to conversations on the Federal Aviation Administration network twenty-four hours a day, seven days a week and would know instantly of a suspected hijacking.[61] As part of Operation Noble Eagle, a joint US-Canadian operation launched after 11 September 2001, Canadian and US forces are monitoring and intercepting all flights of interest within continental North America. In the three years after 9/11 fighter aircraft were sent out more than 1,500 times to determine whether aircraft that did not immediately identify themselves had been hijacked.[62]

Although NORAD's missions have evolved over the years, its command and control system has remained the same. Since its inception NORAD has had a command arrangement designed to maintain Canadian (and US) sovereignty. It is a binational command in which, by tradition, the commander is an American and the deputy commander is a Canadian. As one moves down through the integrated command structure, one sees Canadians at all levels. While primarily a command and control structure, NORAD does have some assigned forces. In this sense it can be contrasted with NORTHCOM, which is a command and control structure without significant assigned forces. But although there are forces assigned operationally to NORAD, these are under its operational *control*, not its operational *command*.

Clearly, understanding the nature of operational command as distinct from operational control is essential to our understanding of sovereignty in a NORAD context, and thus of sovereignty in any possible future NORAD-like arrangement involving land or maritime forces. "Operational command" is the authority granted to a commander to assign missions or tasks to subordinate commanders, to deploy units, or to reassign forces. "Operational control" is much more limited in that authority is granted to a commander only to direct forces to accomplish specific missions or tasks that are usually limited by function, time, or location.[63] Canada, for example, has agreed to have a certain number of aircraft on daily alert within NORAD, but the Canadian government has specified how these aircraft may be used in the event of a crisis. In so doing it has reserved Canada's right to employ its NORAD forces in any way it considers appropriate. Not only has Canada retained operational command of its forces, but it has also ensured its involvement in operational control decisions in the event of a crisis. Aircraft and personnel respond through NORAD's integrated chain of command. Ultimately, NORAD answers equally to the president of the United States and the prime minister of Canada.

Addressing the Airborne Threat

In the evolving security environment Canada and the United States have to be able to track and intercept aircraft approaching North America, or already over North America, and to detect and intercept cruise missiles and unmanned aerial vehicles launched by terrorists or rogue states from international waters close to North America. The threat posed by aircraft approaching or over North America is self-evident in the post-9/11 era. Cruise missiles also represent a growing danger. For terrorist groups operating without the support of a nation-state, such weapons are more easily attainable than ballistic missiles. Moreover, given the US's decision to deploy a limited ballistic missile defence (see chapter 6), those who want to strike North America may seek alternative means of attack, including cruise missiles or aerial drones. Of particular concern is that missiles or drones could be armed with a nuclear, biological, chemical, or radiological warhead and launched from ships off the North American coast.

NORAD gets surveillance and early-warning information about aircraft approaching North America from the North Warning System (NWS) of radars, as well as from coastal radars on the east and west coasts of Canada. Constructed in the late 1980s and early 1990s, the NWS is comprised of fifteen long-range radars (eleven in Canada, four in Alaska) and thirty-nine short-range radars (thirty-six in Canada, three in Alaska) along the seventieth parallel. These radars are located in response to the Cold War polar threat. As a result, Canada has only intermittent surveillance coverage of much of its vast airspace and air approach. Airborne Early Warning and Control System (AWACS) aircraft augment the radar system in times of alert. Yet Canada still has only intermittent surveillance coverage of much of its vast airspace and air approach.[64] Airborne Early Warning and Control System (AWACS) aircraft augment the radar system in times of alert.

Currently, civilian air traffic controllers rely on the signal emitted by an aircraft's transponder to locate aircraft and, should the transponder be turned off, on primary radar returns. But these do not show the aircraft's identity or altitude. Moreover, *The 9/11 Commission Report* revealed the difficulty of finding aircraft that do not identify themselves.[65] Defence experts have argued that NORAD's existing capabilities for the detection of aircraft that do not comply with the rules for identification need to be extended to cover most of North America's land mass.[66] As an initial step, Canada's air force has been tasked with examining the acquisition of additional radars to provide better coverage of population centres and vital areas of infrastructure.[67]

Meanwhile, no system yet exists to continuously monitor the cruise missile threat to North America. The United States uses a patchwork of surveillance systems, including AWACS and navy E-2C aircraft, ship-based Aegis scanners, and land-based radar.[68] The cruise missile threat is a prime motivation for the real-time sharing between Canada and the United States of information on vessels approaching North America – the warning time for a sea-launched cruise missile could be as little as ten minutes.[69]

By the middle of the next decade the United States plans to have in place a space-based radar system that will fill many surveillance gaps. Based in low and medium Earth orbit, the system will be a constellation of between twenty and twenty-five small satellites using a combination of phased-array radars (for tracking) and synthetic-aperture radars (to distinguish objects from their backgrounds) to achieve a ground moving target indication capability.[70] In essence, space-based radar will take to the level of space many of the attributes of the US Air Force's Joint Surveillance Target Attack Radar System (JSTARS) aircraft.[71] Whereas JSTARS can survey hundreds of square miles of terrain for the movement of vehicles through all kinds of weather, space-based radar will be able to watch thousands of square miles, tracking ships and low-flying aircraft or drones as well as cruise missiles approaching North America.

NORAD relies on tactical fighter aircraft to intercept threatening aircraft.[72] Today, in the post-9/11 era, fighter aircraft are more relevant to homeland defence than they have been since bombers were displaced by ballistic missiles as the primary threat to North America in the early 1960s. Since 11 September 2001, as noted earlier, Canadian and US military aircraft have been called out to intercept suspicious aircraft hundreds of times – a steep rise in the handful of intercepts NORAD undertook each year before the terrorist attacks. Canada's current contribution to the air interception mission is four squadrons of CF-18 Hornets. In future, it must ensure that it has an appropriate land-based fighter for its renewed air defence role at home, and that it has enough aircraft on ready alert in the right locations to quickly shadow, and if necessary intercept, threatening aircraft approaching or already over Canada's major cities. Here there are a number of potential shortfalls. The auditor general has questioned whether, in light of new threats to North America, Canada has enough fighters to properly defend Canada and contribute to North American defence.[73] In addition, locations of Canada's fighter bases – Cold Lake, Alberta, and Bagotville, Quebec – are appropriate to yesterday's circumpolar threat; they are too far from the large civilian population centres that are the focus of contemporary threats.[74] This means that a hijacked airliner heading for Toronto, for example, might have to be engaged by US fighters because Canadian fighters are based too far away. Beyond this, existing command and control arrangements in Canada, which require the Canadian government rather than a military commander to order an aircraft shot down, may preclude a rapid response.[75]

Canada and the United States have only a limited ability to defend against cruise missiles. The US Army is making improvements to its Patriot missile, which has capabilities against cruise and short-range ballistic missiles, while the US Navy is extending the capability of its Standard Missile (SM-3) so that it can intercept ballistic and cruise missiles and aircraft.[76] It is also possible that the Canadian army's Air Defence Anti-tank System could be used to destroy cruise missiles, coastal vessels, and aircraft approaching the continent.[77] But increased research and investment in the area of defending against cruise missiles will be necessary. America's Defense Science Board has recommended that NORTHCOM be assigned the task of developing a road map for defending against the low-altitude air threat,[78] while the Pentagon's draft strategy for homeland defence assigns NORAD the responsibility of examining capabilities for rapidly deployable air and cruise missile defences.[79]

Land and Maritime Threats

The nature of the threat to North America in the decades following World War II was such that greater cooperation between the
United States and Canada was needed to handle airborne and
ballistic missile threats to North America. Even after the Cold War
the level of concern remained high, and NORAD's aerospace warning and control mission was maintained. Growing worries about
rogue state ballistic missiles also fed into this assessment. But in
the years leading up to 9/11, US and Canadian intelligence agencies, academia, government agencies, and bipartisan commissions
were most worried about the prospect of terrorists using WMD on
North American soil. The fact that the 9/11 attacks were conventional did nothing to ease concerns about WMD, because the sheer
magnitude of the attacks demonstrated a change in the nature of
terrorism, traced since the mid-1990s from politically motivated
attacks with limited casualties to attacks with ill-defined objectives and mass casualties. As a result, since 9/11 earlier concerns
about the terrorist use of weapons of mass destruction have only
grown stronger.

The threat to North America today is such that it is driving
increased Canada-US cooperation in addressing land and maritime threats to North America. Specific scenarios might include a
WMD terrorist attack somewhere along the Canada-US land border
or on a border-spanning bridge; terrorists could also plant a nuclear
device on a container ship headed for a major North American
port or use an offshore trawler to launch a biochemical attack. In
the months following 9/11 there were numerous reports that
Canada and the US were considering the creation of a command
that would oversee not only the air forces guarding North America
(currently NORAD's mandate), but also land and maritime forces
charged with this mission. But this prospect prompted an outcry
in Canada, especially among members of the Liberal Cabinet.
The government responded by insisting that Canada was not
being asked to join America's new Northern Command, nor was
it actively considering any new NORAD-like command that would
include land and maritime forces. High-level bilateral negotiations
ensued, and in 2002 the two countries announced an agreement
to establish a Canada-US planning group to examine increased
Canada-US land and maritime military cooperation for the defence
of North America.

Created in 2003, the Canada-US Planning Group is co-located with NORAD headquarters in Colorado Springs and is headed by NORAD's deputy commander. It comprises about fifty officers, half American and half Canadian, and it is charged with:

- Preparing contingency plans for jointly deploying military forces within North America in the event of a crisis, including terrorist attacks and natural disasters;
- Coordinating the sharing of maritime surveillance and intelligence information to give leaders in both countries a comprehensive threat assessment;
- Coordinating and stepping up joint military exercises between the Canadian and American armies and navies to help them deter threats and respond to crises; and
- Improving the military's links and standard operating procedures with police and other emergency services in the civilian world.

Although the stated objective of establishing the binational planning group was to work out the details of a coordinated response in advance of a crisis, in fact many of the important decisions were hammered out in the months before the group was created. Rather than relying on a set of operating procedures, as NORAD would in dealing with an aerospace threat, the binational planning group would evaluate each emergency on a case-by-case basis. Unlike NORAD, the binational planning group would have no standing forces assigned to it. It would be a permanent headquarters organization that could call on forces from the different services as required. In the event of a crisis, any Canada-US military force called up by the planning group would remain under the operational control of the home country – that is, under Canadian operational control if within Canada, and under American operational control if within the United States. This situation stands in contrast with that of NORAD, in which the operational control of a fighter aircraft does not change when the aircraft crosses the border. Overall, the binational planning group was presented as an alternative to formally joining the US military's Northern Command or to creating some sort of "super-NORAD" military structure.

Since that time it has become clear that these decisions were not set in stone – they have continued to evolve. The binational planning group is not so much an established entity as a planning team working on the details of some future entity. One idea being discussed is a "North American version of NATO" that would see NORAD adapted into an integrated military command encompassing land, sea and air operations.[80] Another idea is the creation of a Canada-US maritime command, modelled on NORAD and including an integrated command structure, to protect against coastal terror attacks.[81] This alternative reflects the view that an integrated maritime arrangement with the US makes sense, but not necessarily one based on an expanded NORAD, since the binational maritime defence of North America involves what are, in essence, two separate theatres of operation.[82] Moreover, important questions need to be answered as to how an expanded NORAD would relate to Northern Command and Canada Command, since it is difficult to imagine these commands standing aside while a new binational command responds to a crisis.[83]

Increased Canada-US institutional cooperation is logical and governed by response time and geography. In light of this it is important to ask how much time we need to respond effectively to a land or maritime threat to North America. NORAD was established because Canadian and US security demanded a near-instantaneous response to air and, later, aerospace threats to the continent. Forces and command arrangements had to be in place in advance, because the interval between detection and response was, and is, literally only minutes. Land and maritime threats to North America do not travel so quickly, but they are unique in that they are generated by terrorists who are difficult to detect. Moreover, they could involve rapidly spreading and highly lethal weapons of mass destruction. There may be very little time to assess the nature of the threat and decide on an appropriate response, particularly when it comes to land-based threats or maritime threats close to shore. Because most of Canada's population lives close to the Canada-US border, any threat to it is likely to materialize within a few hundred miles of the frontier. This, combined with the fact that the threat knows no borders, means that US interests would likely be directly involved in the event of a crisis. Even if the threat were confined to Canada, geography dictates that backup could more quickly arrive from south of the border than from other areas of Canada.

Decisions on the final institutional mechanism to encompass increased Canada-US military cooperation for the land and maritime defence of North America will likely figure in the 2006 NORAD renewal. Any expanded Canada-US military institutional arrangement to cover land- and sea-based threats to North America should include some command procedures that are similar to those of NORAD. The agreement's command and control arrangements protect Canadian sovereignty and give Canada a much greater voice in continental defence affairs than would otherwise be the case. If NORAD were transformed into a North American (maritime, land, and aerospace) defence command, then the requirement established under the binational planning group that each situation be assessed on case-by-case basis would be unnecessary once possible scenarios and contingency plans were fully developed by the planning group. Every situation is different, of course, and each will inevitably require a crisis-specific solution, but developing a set of standard operating procedures for various contingencies can only enhance the prospect of an effective military response. For similar reasons, an integrated military command with limited standing forces in place for responding to land and maritime threats would also make sense. Both solutions would also enhance the military's ability to support civilian-led homeland security missions.

But the Canadian government must continue to insist that land or maritime forces be deployed under the operational control of the home country. In the current NORAD framework, American fighters could cross the border into Canada and still be under the operational control of an American officer. This framework is not sufficient in terms of Canadian sovereignty when it comes to maritime, and especially land force, responses to threats to North America. "When stripped to its bare essentials," points out one scholar, "sovereignty is the ability of an identifiable group of people to control what happens within a specific geographic region."[84] If a land force unit is sent to respond to a WMD disaster in Windsor, then a Canadian officer must be in charge; if a ship suspected of transporting a nuclear device enters Canadian waters off Vancouver, then a Canadian vessel must be in operational control. Both scenarios would directly affect US security, and it can be assumed that the United States would undertake to carry out the operation if Canada were militarily unable to do so. Clearly, the old adage "If we don't secure our own territory, then the Americans will do it for us" would be highly relevant in such situations. It is imperative – both in terms of sovereignty and security – for Canada to maintain sufficient military forces to take control of these sorts of operations.

CONCLUSION

The post-9/11 security environment is arguably driving the Canada-US defence relationship to be more closely integrated than it has been at any other point in history. No longer confined to the aerospace dimension, Canada-US cooperation for the defence of North America is expanding to the land and maritime dimensions. Canada will have to establish firm positions in certain areas; most notably, it must require that maritime and land forces operate under Canadian control on Canadian territory and in Canadian territorial waters. It will also have to ensure that it has the forces and capabilities to back up its positions. The next chapter turns to a particular aspect of homeland defence, and one that is closely linked to the future of NORAD: space and ballistic missile defence.

6

Space and Ballistic Missile Defence

It is not too much of a stretch to date the issue of Canada's possible involvement in an American-led ballistic missile defence (BMD) system back to the Soviet launch of *Sputnik* in October 1957. Because it was a satellite propelled into orbit atop a multi-stage missile, *Sputnik* not only marked the beginning of the space age but was also a vivid indication that the Soviet Union was on the verge of developing long-range ballistic missiles. The United States immediately set about getting its own satellite, *Explorer I*, into orbit, but it turned its attention to ballistic missiles as well. By early 1958 offensive and defensive long-range missile development had become a priority in the United States.[1]

Space and ballistic missile defence are two separate issues, but they have so many linkages that it is difficult to discuss them in isolation. Long-range ballistic missiles pass through space (but do not go into orbit). Some sensors designed to detect ballistic missiles can also track satellites, while others can detect terrestrial projectiles, like scud missiles. Conversely, systems designed to track satellites and space objects can also be used to detect incoming ballistic missiles. These linkages have been reflected in the mission and responsibilities of the North American Aerospace Defense Command (NORAD) almost from the outset. Since the early 1960s NORAD has been mandated with detecting and warning of aircraft and ballistic missiles, intercepting aircraft, and tracking space objects. In 1996 NORAD's mission was formally stated as aerospace warning and aerospace control, opening the possibility of a role for NORAD in ballistic missile defence.

NORAD's role in the surveillance and control of North American airspace was discussed in chapter 5. This chapter examines the other elements of NORAD's mission – ballistic missile early warning and space surveillance, and the implications of Canada's decision not to participate in America's ballistic missile defence system. It begins by outlining technological developments in ballistic missile early warning systems and space surveillance systems over the past half-century. It then gives a brief overview of the various US initiatives to create a missile defence capability, including the most recent undertaking, before looking more closely at command and control arrangements. It concludes that ballistic missile early warning, space surveillance, and ballistic missile defence are difficult to separate. Canada's decision to allow ballistic missile early warning information to flow from NORAD to the US ballistic missile defence system but not to participate in the system itself has the potential to increasingly limit Canada's access to America's space-related information. The decision guarantees that Canada would have no role in determining the nature of the response to an incoming missile, but it could also create a situation where Canada has limited or no knowledge of the missile threat in the first place. Both scenarios represent a decline in Canadian sovereignty and security.

BALLISTIC MISSILE EARLY WARNING SYSTEMS

The United States responded to the launch of *Sputnik* by constructing the Ballistic Missile Early Warning System (BMEWS), beginning in 1958. Giant radars built at sites in Alaska, Greenland, and England became operational in the early 1960s, providing the capability to detect ballistic missiles coming over the polar ice cap and giving the United States a fifteen-minute attack warning. They also provided tracking data on most orbiting satellites. None of the sites for this system were on Canadian territory; nor did Canada contribute financially to the enterprise. Nonetheless, the decision was made to channel all the ballistic missile surveillance information to the commander of NORAD, and the elaborate BMEWS computer and display facilities were installed at NORAD headquarters.[2] Beginning in the 1970s the mechanical BMEWS radars, which required several people to operate and could only track one object at a time, were replaced with Solid State Phased-Array

Radar Systems (sspars), which could maintain tracks on multiple objects simultaneously. Also at this time, the United States established two Phased-Array Warning System sites further south – one on Cape Cod and the other on the coast of California – that used the sspars technology to monitor the growing threat of missiles fired from Soviet submarines.

Ground-based radars are one means by which NORAD and the US Air Force have monitored the ballistic missile threat over the years. But even by the early 1960s technology had progressed to the point that a space-based infrared system could reliably detect missile launches. The Missile Defense Alarm System (MIDAS) was a successful program that explored the use of long-wave infrared sensors to detect missile launches and meet what was perceived to be a growing Soviet intercontinental ballistic missile threat. In 1962 MIDAS was reorganized as a long-term research and development effort that eventually yielded the Defence Support Program (DSP) system of satellites. The DSP satellite system consists of between eight and ten satellites at any one time, the first of which was launched in 1971. Operating some 37,000 kilometres above the Earth's surface in geosynchronous, or high-Earth, orbit, [3] the system provides strategic and tactical missile-launch warnings by detecting the infrared radiation in a missile's exhaust trail.[4] Although the system was designed to pick up intercontinental ballistic missile launches, it has also proven useful for other applications, such as detecting Iraqi Scud missile launches during the 1991 Gulf War.

The US Air Force is in the process of acquiring a new generation of space-based sensors to detect ballistic missiles, with plans to deploy a Space-Based Infrared System (SBIRS) of satellites in high- and low-Earth orbit. SBIRS High, consisting of four satellites operating in geosynchronous orbit and two in highly elliptical orbit, will replace the DSP satellite system to provide strategic and tactical information on ballistic missile launches. SBIRS Low, now renamed the Space Tracking and Surveillance System (STSS), will consist of at least twenty satellites operating in low-Earth orbit.[5] Using onboard infrared sensors, the STSS satellites – the first of which are scheduled for launch in 2006–07 – will be able to detect, track, and discriminate ballistic missiles throughout their trajectories.[6]

Beyond this, the US Navy is also moving into ballistic missile early warning systems. The Pentagon is in the process of installing a giant X-Band radar – weighing 50,000 tons – on a self-propelled oil-rig platform. Once the radar is installed, the platform will be sailed to the North Pacific and based in the Aleutian Islands. Its role will be to pick up tracking information on long-range ballistic missiles and provide this information to land-based interceptors.[7] The US Navy is also modifying fifteen destroyers and three Aegis cruisers to operate in the Sea of Japan and provide ballistic missile early warning information to the ground-based system being established in Alaska (discussed later).[8]

SPACE SURVEILLANCE SYSTEMS

Almost as soon as the United States began deploying its BMEWS radars, it grew concerned that because they could only detect ballistic missiles coming at North America from over the polar ice cap, the radars might end up being some sort of Maginot Line that the Soviet Union could go around by launching a ballistic missiles from southern regions or from space.[9] The individual US military services moved quickly to develop sensor systems that could track space objects coming from all directions. In 1958 the US Navy established a space surveillance system known as SPASUR, an electronic fence stretching across the southern United States.[10] Meanwhile, the US Air Force set up a worldwide network of radars and space-probing cameras called Spacetrack. In 1960 the Space Detection and Tracking System, or SPADATS, was formed to bring these systems together under a single military management. Like BMEWS, SPADATS was placed under the operational control of NORAD.

In subsequent years the network expanded to include two Canadian sites (now disbanded), at St Margarets, New Brunswick, and Cold Lake, Alberta, each equipped with a Baker-Nunn satellite-tracking camera. In the early 1980s a number of space-tracking radars were added to the SPADATS network, notably the Pacific Barrier System of sites in Southeast Asia. Later that decade the US Air Force replaced the old Baker-Nunn cameras with the Electro-optical Deep Space Surveillance System, featuring ground-based telescope sensors linked to a video camera. It also added more tracking sites. Today the US space surveillance network includes army-, navy-, and air-force-operated ground-based radars and optical sensors located at more than twenty-five sites around the world (including the BMEWS sites). Using a combination of phased-array radars, conventional radars, and deep space surveillance telescopes, the network is mandated with detecting and tracking space objects and predicting when and where a decaying space object will re-enter the Earth's atmosphere.

As was the case with the original SPADATS, the expanded US space surveillance network remains a primarily land-based system. The only space-based component is an experimental US space sensor that was launched in 1996 and is coming to the end of its operational life.[11] Significantly, Canada is spending $65 million to develop a capability to gather space-based sensor information. Under Project Sapphire the Department of National Defence (DND) is building a satellite with an optical sensor that will be able to look at objects in deep space, approximately 6,000 to 40,000 kilometres from Earth. Scheduled for deployment in 2009 or 2010, Sapphire will gather information on foreign satellites and track space debris then feed this data into America's surveillance network.[12] Although Sapphire is primarily meant to keep tabs on the hundreds of pieces of space junk that are orbiting the Earth and that occasionally crash through the atmosphere, it will also have application to ballistic missiles. By determining whether or not a space object is a ballistic missile in mid-course phase, Sapphire could provide an indirect contribution to America's ballistic missile defence program.

Sapphire is a key component of Canada's Joint Space Capability, a DND project that centres on two space-related capabilities: surveillance of space (from the ground or from space) and surveillance from space (downward at the Earth).[13] The Joint Space Capability, in turn, is part of the Joint Space Project, a planned $600 million investment in co-operation with the United States in space-related areas. Led by the Directorate of Space Development at National Defence Headquarters, the project involves examining a range of options for how Canada might contribute to America's space surveillance network.[14] Beyond those assigned to Sapphire, other funds allocated within the Joint Space Project include $7 million for the definition phase of a ground-based optical sensor system, and $13 million to launch two microsatellites into space. Dubbed High Earth Orbit Space Surveillance, this project uses microsatellites, weighing only seventy kilograms each, designed to track foreign satellites and asteroids. Like Sapphire, this project will feed information into the US space surveillance network.[15] Another space-related project, and one that falls into the category of surveillance from space, is Project Polar Epsilon, which is a plan to buy time on a commercial satellite system to gain space-based surveillance information about Canada's Arctic land mass (see chapter 5).

BALLISTIC MISSILE DEFENCE SYSTEMS

America's interest in ballistic missile defences predates even the first intercontinental ballistic missile. The United States began exploring the idea of ballistic missile defence in the late 1940s, but it was not until the launch of *Sputnik* that its efforts became more focused. The earliest American anti-ballistic missile (ABM) was the Nike Zeus, developed in the late 1950s for the point defence of army units. Despite being a US Army system, the Nike Zeus was strongly supported at the time by the commander of NORAD, who, even in those early days, believed that it was fruitless to have air defences (through NORAD) without being able to defend against ballistic missiles. By 1960, only two years after NORAD had been established as an integrated binational air defence organization, the US commander of NORAD had declared the organization's first priority to be ballistic missile defence.[16] Concerned that the Soviet Union could deploy nuclear warheads on satellites over US territory, the US Air Force pressed for a satellite interception system, and in 1964 a rudimentary ground-based anti-satellite capability was established on a remote Pacific island. Other experimental anti-ballistic missile systems included the US Army's Sprint-Spartan ABM, developed in the late 1960s as a defence against accidental Soviet launch and the threat from China, and its Safeguard ABM system, which used a nuclear-armed missile as its interceptor and was actually deployed operationally for a brief period in 1975–76 at a site in North Dakota.

US statements and activities with respect to ballistic missile defence in the early 1960s did not receive much attention in Canada, whose public and politicians were much more caught up in the issue of arming the US Air Force's Bomarc missile – designed to target Soviet bombers, not ballistic missiles – with nuclear warheads. But in the latter part of the decade Canadian officials became concerned that the United States might want to build ABM sites in Canada and/or pursue nuclear warheads for its ABMs. At the time of the 1968 NORAD renewal agreement, Canada insisted on, and succeeded in getting, a clause stating that Canada would not be obliged to participate in any future BMD system. Regardless of the clause, in the following years the issue of BMD declined in importance on the Canada-US defence relations agenda. In 1972 the United States and the Soviet Union signed the Anti-ballistic Missile Treaty, which precluded nationwide missile defences by stating that each side could deploy only two (amended to one in 1974) ABM sites. The treaty was intended to ensure mutual vulnerability to nuclear weapons, remove incentives to build more weapons to overcome adversary defences, and therefore to contribute to deterrence and strategic stability. The United States built its treaty-compliant ABM site in North Dakota in the mid-1970s but abandoned it almost immediately because of the cost and lack of military effectiveness. Russia's ABM system, which surrounds Moscow and employs technology similar to that of Safeguard, remains nominally in operation.

The existence of the ABM Treaty, combined with the absence of an American BMD system, persuaded Canada to drop the BMD clause in 1981.[17] That year Canada also accepted a change in the NORAD agreement, such that the organization became the North American Aerospace Defense Command – a formal recognition of the fact that NORAD had been involved in aerospace activities almost since its inception. Ironically, less than two years later President Ronald Reagan made his dramatic speech announcing the Strategic Defense Initiative (SDI). In his March 1983 address Reagan asked, "What if free people could live secure in the knowledge that their security did not rest upon the threat of instant US retaliation to deter a Soviet attack, that we could intercept and destroy ballistic missiles before they reached our own soil or that of our allies?"[18] The president was, in effect, turning the offence/defence debate on its head, arguing that the best way to guarantee North American security was not offensively, through mutual assured destruction, but defensively, through ballistic missile defences. His answer – an elaborate system of futuristic weapons like orbital particle beam stations and space-based kinetic kill vehicles to fend off a massive Soviet ballistic missile attack – soon became known as "Star Wars."

The SDI announcement took America and its allies by surprise; Reagan had not even consulted most of his own officials. It triggered a few years of furious activity, as US officials tried to implement

Reagan's vision. Research programs were established, and allies were asked to participate. In Canada it sparked a fierce debate that was not resolved until 1985, when the Conservative government of Brian Mulroney decided that it would sign no government-to-government co-operative agreement, but that Canadian firms could participate and compete for contracts under existing bilateral defence development and production-sharing agreements. It was not long, however, before BMD once again declined in importance as a Canada-US issue. Technological challenges and the end of the Cold War led to congressional funding cuts and a dramatic scaling back of the original SDI vision.

The 1991 Gulf War and the performance of the Patriot missile led to a refocusing of BMD research towards defences against shorter-range missiles and the protection of American and allied forces deployed abroad. The administration of George Bush Sr announced its intention to focus on a system called Global Protection against Limited Strikes (GPALS), which would be less than half the size of even the Phase I component of the old SDI. Rather than protect the United States against an all-out Soviet missile attack, GPALS would protect US and allied deployed forces, as well as US and allied territory, against limited ballistic missile strikes, accidental or otherwise. Sensors would be based on land and in space (as had been the case for decades), while interceptors could be ground-, sea-, or space-based.[19]

Under the Clinton administration SDI continued to be refocused. Congress scaled back the funds allocated to ballistic missile defence but at the same time supported continuing research into a limited National Missile Defence (NMD) system for the continental United States. The plan envisaged under Clinton centred on protecting all of the US states (including Alaska and Hawaii) against a small number of missiles from rogue states or an accidental launch by Russia or China using land-based interceptors against missiles in their mid-course phase. In 1996 the US formally adopted the "three plus three" approach to developing a ballistic missile defence capability – within three years the country would attain the technological capability to field an NMD system and then be in a position to put the system in place within three years of any decision, based on the threat, to go ahead with deployment.

Throughout much of the 1990s US authorities believed that no new intercontinental ballistic missile threat to North America would emerge for many years. But in 1998 the Commission to Assess the Ballistic Missile Threat to the United States, chaired by Donald Rumsfeld, stated in a report to Congress that North Korea and Iran could possess intercontinental ballistic missiles within as little as five years, and Iraq within ten years. Moreover, it argued that during several of those years the United States might not be aware that these countries were pursuing a ballistic missile capability. The ability of intelligence agencies to monitor the emerging threat was eroding as nations became increasingly sophisticated at concealing evidence of ballistic missile activity and gained greater access to technical assistance from outside sources. The conclusions of the Rumsfeld report, which was released in July 1998, were reinforced the following month, when North Korea test-fired a new longer-range missile over Japanese territory. Within six months the Clinton administration had announced that the rate of proliferation had reached the point at which the threat criterion had been met, and that deployment should go ahead once the technology criterion was also fulfilled.[20] The 1999 National Missile Defense Act, signed by President Clinton and strongly supported by congressional Democrats and Republicans alike, *requires* the United States to implement a system to protect against limited attacks "as soon as technologically possible." But the president did not decide, as required by the three-plus-three formula, to go ahead with NMD deployment. This was primarily due to ongoing concerns about the technological feasibility of such a system. In the fall of 2000 Clinton deferred for the next administration the decision of whether to pass beyond research and development to the deployment stage of ballistic missile defence.

The administration of George Bush Jr entered office strongly in favour of ballistic missile defences. In its view the US-Russian strategic framework, as embodied in the 1972 ABM Treaty, was no longer appropriate to contemporary realities. The treaty served to reinforce Cold War threat perceptions that were no longer relevant in the post–Cold War era, and it limited America's ability to respond to the new threat environment. Depending on one's perspective, the terrorist attacks of 11 September 2001 either reinforced the perceived need for, or demonstrated the irrelevance of, ballistic missile defences. While some pointed out that an effective missile defence system over the United States would have done little to stop planes from flying into buildings, others argued that the attacks only served to highlight that anything is possible, including rogue state ballistic missile attacks. Concurring with the latter view, President Bush announced three months after the attacks that the US would withdraw from the ABM Treaty (effective six months later).

Throughout 2002 the newly created Missile Defense Agency built and tested mobile and sea-based sensors that detect and track missiles, and it conducted tests with short-range missile defence systems that had been prohibited by the ABM Treaty. While one test failed, four were successful.[21] Meanwhile, late in 2002 North Korea revealed that it had been secretly developing uranium-based nuclear weapons and would restart nuclear reactors that had been shut down under a 1994 agreement negotiated by the Clinton administration. The potential for technical feasibility and new developments in the international security environment prompted Bush to make the decision, in December 2002, to begin deploying a limited ballistic missile defence system.

The BMD system envisaged by the Bush administration in the long term goes well beyond that which was foreseen by the Clinton administration. Broadened from National Missile Defense to Global Ballistic Missile Defense, the system will be designed to protect the continental United States as well as allied territory and American and allied deployed forces, much like the GPALS system of the early 1990s. The Bush team seeks to put in place a multi-layered missile defence system that will engage missiles in all three phases of flight (rather than just the mid-course phase) using land-, sea-, air-, and space-based interceptors (rather than just land-based interceptors). More specifically, the Missile Defense Agency seeks to develop a system to shoot down missiles during the following phases: the boost phase, from launch to the completion of propulsion fuel burn, using airborne, space-based, or sea-based interceptors; the mid-course phase, outside the atmosphere, using ground- and sea-based interceptors; and the terminal phase, when the missile re-enters the atmosphere, using ground-based interceptors. Currently, the primary emphasis is on land- and sea-based interceptors, and to a certain extent airborne interceptors, like the airborne laser.[22] But the Missile Defense Agency is also pursuing technology for space-based interceptors, which would be particularly useful for destroying a ballistic missile in its boost phase. Budget documents indicate the Pentagon would like the Missile Defense Agency to have a test version of a space-based interceptor ready by 2012.[23]

Although the United States has ambitious long-term goals, its immediate plans are quite limited and in fact are very similar to the Clinton administration's plans. By the end of 2005 the Pentagon is to have in place twenty ground-based interceptors at sites in Fort Greely, Alaska, and Vandenberg Air Force Base in California, and another twenty interceptors on Navy Aegis cruisers. The sea-based BMD system is to provide, by 2006, a defence against short-, medium-, and intermediate-range ballistic missiles,[24] while the land-based system is to target long-range, or intercontinental, ballistic missiles in their mid-course phase.[25]

The fact that the present administration has made ballistic missile defence a priority does not mean that a dramatic new technological situation in this area has suddenly presented itself. In fact, there is much dispute over whether a BMD system is technologically possible at this time.[26] Although successful, the tests thus far have been criticized by the US General Accounting Office as being "repetitive and scripted" because they have failed to fully simulate the speed and altitude of a real-life enemy missile. Even the rudimentary ground-based sites established in 2004 are generally considered to be a developmental program due to a lack of concrete evidence that they would actually work.[27] The United States pursued BMD in the 1960s but abandoned it in the 1970s because of technological unfeasibility. In the 1980s President Reagan announced a grand design for ballistic missile defence, but within a few years it was set aside because it was beyond technological reach. President Clinton signed the National Missile Defense Act, which requires the US to implement a BMD system as soon as technologically possible, but technology did not make it possible, and Clinton deferred a deployment decision to the next administration. President Bush has decided to proceed with a BMD system, but it remains very difficult to "hit a bullet with a bullet." In the coming years the United States could decide that its resources would be better spent elsewhere, particularly when it comes to the development of costly and technologically challenging space-based interceptors.

Nonetheless, a new situation has presented itself. "The general idea of getting [a BMD] capability has always been there," notes a senior Missile Defense Agency official, "but it has never been approved with long-term program planning and budgets behind it."[28] It seems apparent that, at a minimum, a ballistic missile defence system comprised of land-, sea-, and space-based sensors, and land- and sea-based interceptors, is set to become a permanent feature of North American homeland defence. Historically, Canada has resisted invitations to participate in America's ballistic missile defence programs partly out of concern that a BMD system might set off a new arms race. It believed that Russia and possibly China would respond to a missile defence shield by building more missiles in the hope that at least some would get through. This concern was largely removed when America withdrew from the ABM Treaty in 2002 and the action elicited only muted criticism from Russia and China, although questions remain in this area.[29]

Canada has also resisted participation in ballistic missile defence because it is against the weaponization of space. The crux of the issue is the differing US and Canadian interpretations of the 1967 Outer Space Treaty, of which both Canada and the United States are signatories. The only activity the Outer Space Treaty explicitly forbids is "the orbiting of nuclear weapons or other weapons of mass destruction, their installation on celestial bodies, or the stationing of such weapons in outer space in any other manner." Beyond this, the treaty permits the "peaceful use" of outer space in accordance with "international law, including the Charter of the United Nations." Canada has focused on the "peaceful use" component and interpreted it to mean that outer space can only be used for non-aggressive purposes, such as surveillance and communications. The US, by contrast, has focused on the reference to the UN Charter. Because article 51 of the charter recognizes the inherent right of self-defence, the Outer Space Treaty is interpreted as permitting those outer space missions necessary for national security, including not only surveillance and communications but also the application of military force from space-based weapons.

Command Arrangements

In the almost five decades since NORAD was created the command arrangements pertaining to NORAD's ballistic missile warning and space surveillance mission have essentially remained the same, although the names and mandates of organizations on the American side have changed. Decisions about BMEWS and SPADATS established the practice whereby the relevant US command has retained operational command of information, but NORAD maintains operational control.[30] Ballistic missile detection and space surveillance information is gathered by the US-only command, but this information is channelled into NORAD for assessment and early warning.

From 1954, when US Continental Air Defense Command (CONAD) was created, until 1975, when it was disestablished, operational command of the early warning and space surveillance functions rested with CONAD and one of its component commands, Air Defense Command (another CONAD component command was Army Air Defense Command). Air Defense Command, which was renamed Aerospace Defense Command in 1968, formed the US contribution to NORAD. The provision of information to NORAD was facilitated by the fact that the commander of CONAD was also the commander of NORAD.

Beginning in the mid-1970s, a number of important US military organizational changes took place. When CONAD was disestablished Aerospace Defense Command was reorganized to incorporate the functions formerly carried out by CONAD. Then, in 1979, administrative control of the missile warning and space surveillance sites was transferred to Strategic Air Command, which controlled America's long-range bombers. It was not long before this situation, which left most other space systems scattered among different agencies, was found to be unsatisfactory. In 1982 the Pentagon created US Air Force Space Command, a major command on a par with Strategic Air Command that brought together all air force space assets. But this decision, too, was insufficient because it did not incorporate the space assets of the US Army and the US Navy. Finally, in 1985 the Pentagon created US Space Command (SPACECOM), a unified command encompassing all US military space assets, including the missile warning and space surveillance systems of US Air Force Space Command that supported NORAD. SPACECOM headquarters was co-located with that of NORAD at Peterson Air Force Base in Colorado Springs. Also at this time, the Pentagon clarified US Space Command's relationship with NORAD: Space Command would provide missile warning and space surveillance data to NORAD as necessary to fulfill America's commitment to the NORAD agreement. This arrangement, once again, was facilitated by the fact that the commander of Space Command was double-hatted as the commander of NORAD.

Strategic Air Command was disestablished in 1992, and on the same day Strategic Command (STRATCOM) came into being. It brought together command and control of all three arms of America's nuclear triad – intercontinental ballistic missiles, submarine-launched ballistic missiles, and the long-range bomber force. The creation of this new command was not directly relevant to Canada and NORAD until 2002, when Space Command ceased to exit and its functions were transferred to STRATCOM, which is headquartered at Offutt Air Force Base in Nebraska. Northern Command was also created at this time, and it is headquartered at Peterson Air Force Base; the commander of NORTHCOM is double-hatted as the commander of NORAD (see chapter 5). These new command arrangements mean that NORAD no longer enjoys as direct a relationship as it once did – with CONAD from 1957 to 1975, and with SPACECOM from 1985 to 2002 – with the US command that controls American space assets. Although NORAD continues to receive information from STRATCOM about ballistic missile launches and trajectories and events in space, the new arrangements could make access to US military space planning and operations more difficult for the Canadian military.[31]

The Bush administration's decision to deploy a ballistic missile defence system has necessitated further changes in the US command system as it relates to NORAD. US Strategic Command has overall responsibility for early warning of, and defence against, a missile attack on America and its allies,[32] while Northern Command has been assigned the missile defence mission for North America.[33] Continuing the practice that was established in the early years of NORAD, information from America's ballistic missile early warning systems and space surveillance network is gathered by the US-only command, in this case STRATCOM, and channelled to NORAD for interpretation and assessment so that it can carry out its ballistic missile early warning and space surveillance missions. All of these information-gathering systems, with the exception of the space surveillance systems now being developed by Canada – Sapphire and High Earth Orbit Space Surveillance, noted earlier – are US systems. Canada has no ballistic missile early warning systems. In 2004 Canada and the United States agreed that NORAD would provide its ballistic missile early warning information to NORTHCOM so that it could carry out its ballistic missile defence responsibilities.

In February 2005 the Canadian government decided that Canada would not participate in America's BMD system. The long-term implications of this decision, if any, are as yet unclear. The official US position is that the decision will not change NORAD's long-standing early warning and space surveillance mission. The command's provision, agreed to in 2004, of ballistic missile early warning information to NORTHCOM for ballistic missile defence – like NORAD's decades-long provision of early warning information to America's strategic nuclear command – is considered a viable long-term situation.[34] But others make the case that it is difficult, if not impossible, to divide the warning of, and response to, ballistic missiles. "Battle management of the missile-defence system will be closely linked to providing warning and assessment. Physically, it will all take place in the same room."[35] From this perspective, the organization that has operational control of missile warning and detection should also be in control of the missile defence system, since in the event of an attack there would be only minutes to assess the threat and attempt an interception. Given the close links between ballistic missile early warning, space surveillance, and ballistic missile defence, the US could possibly set up an assessment system parallel to that provided by NORAD and "gradually ease" Canada out of access to information derived from America's ballistic missile early warning and space surveillance systems[36] – with or without Canada's knowledge.

If this were to happen, then NORAD would decline in stature, but it would not disappear because it would still be involved in the surveillance and control of North American airspace. Indeed, the threat posed by civilian airliners and concerns about cruise missiles have ensured the continued relevance of the air defence mission. NORAD would also have an increased role in continental security if its responsibilities were expanded to include the maritime and land defence of North America (see chapter 5).

Canada's decision not to participate in America's BMD system represents a decline in Canadian sovereignty. Although the ballistic missile threat to North America is considered low, it does exist, and it may be on the rise. In the coming years the range and accuracy of ballistic missiles available to proliferators will likely improve, and access to the weapons of mass destruction that make these delivery vehicles so dangerous will continue to spread. In the best-case scenario, Canada will know that a missile is coming but will not have a role in deciding or influencing the nature of the response. Ottawa will not be able to guarantee, for example, that an incoming missile is shot down over the Arctic Ocean as opposed to northern Ontario.[37] Moreover, Canada has lost its ability to ensure that the US system affords Canadian territory the same degree of protection as America's. Critics contend that Canada would not have had a voice in such things in any case; by refusing to participate, however, Canada has guaranteed this state of affairs.

In the worst-case scenario, NORAD's ballistic missile early warning and space surveillance mission would atrophy. Canada could ultimately have limited or no knowledge of a missile coming at its territory, and it could be progressively cut out of access to information from America's Space Surveillance Network, inseparable as it is from the ballistic missile early warning function. Tactically, Canada could no longer be privy to the vast amount of space-related information pertaining to its own space approaches. Strategically, Canada could lose its privileged access to such information about developments around the world. "The idea of us being able to leverage small investments such as Radarsat and Sapphire into bigger and bigger knowledge is pretty well dead in the water now," argues one missile defence expert. "I think they'll shut the doors on us."[38]

CONCLUSION

Almost since its inception, NORAD has been closely involved in the two interrelated missions of ballistic missile early warning and space surveillance. These tasks are arguably inseparable: systems dedicated to ballistic missile warning are also relevant to NORAD's space surveillance and tracking mission; conversely, those systems dedicated to space surveillance and tracking have important applications to ballistic missile early warning. Throughout the Cold War these missions were important to the homeland defence of North America in that they were to warn of a ballistic missile attack, allowing the US to launch a retaliatory strike. Today time may be even more of the essence, because the intention is to intercept an incoming missile rather than to absorb an attack and respond in kind. Canada's decision to allow ballistic missile early warning information to flow from NORAD to the ballistic missile defence system controlled by NORTHCOM but not to participate in the system itself may be a sufficient arrangement in the short to medium term. But the long-term potential impact may be to progressively reduce NORAD's role in ballistic missile early warning and space surveillance, and thus also to reduce Canada's privileged access to the tactical and strategic picture of the world provided by these almost exclusively American systems.

Chapter 7 turns to the third quadrant of requirements for Canadian security and defence – military forces for combating the threat to Canada far from its shores in overseas theatres of operation.

7

Military Requirements for Addressing Threats to the Homeland Abroad

Canada's Standing Committee on National Defence and Veterans Affairs has accurately pointed out that it is not possible to evaluate the operational readiness, or even the relevance, of a military force unless one knows what its expected missions are. Certainly, the Canadian Forces must be able to carry out homeland defence activities and contribute to civilian-led homeland security missions. But the defence of North America also requires an ability to deploy military forces overseas. The committee states this in terms of being able to make a "meaningful contribution" to United Nations, NATO, or coalition operations.[1] A number of editorials on the subject share the view that Canada should spend more on defence because Canadians want to make a difference, and because such spending would rehabilitate Canada's standing as a leading international citizen.[2] Along similar lines, the Conservative Party's vision is "to realize Canada's potential as a leading nation," while that of the Liberals is for Canada to see its "place of pride and influence in the world restored."[3]

Quite apart from Canada's role in the world and its desire to promote a particular set of values, however, there is a Canadian security argument to be made with respect to the ability of the Canadian Forces to participate in military missions far from home. The nature of the threat to North America today is such that its origins are most often found abroad. CSIS points out that many of Canada's security preoccupations originate overseas, making it imperative to identify and understand developments abroad that could become homeland issues. It notes that the initially promising geopolitical developments of the early 1990s gave way to ethnic and religious conflicts, producing instability and creating a climate favourable to terrorism. The result is that today, "religious, political, ideological, and territorial agendas continue to drive terrorist activities, and remain largely associated with the extension of foreign conflict."[4]

Addressing threats to North America abroad may or may not involve a military response. Officials in Canada and the United States have stressed that tackling international terrorism requires action on a number of fronts, including diplomatic, humanitarian, and financial. "We recognize," states official British defence policy, "that we have a range of powerful non-military tools which will often be the first choice to help achieve our aims."[5] Nonetheless, there will be circumstances in which the use of military force will be assessed as necessary. When it comes to military responses overseas, Canadian security will require the CF to be able to participate in two broad types of mission: warfighting, or find-and-strike, operations; and stabilization operations. Each demands a military force with a particular set of characteristics, some of which overlap. Moreover, it is conceivable that both types of operation, as well as a humanitarian assistance mission, could take place in roughly the same location, just a few blocks apart. The chief of defence staff has referred to this "complex and chaotic operational environment" as a "3 block war."[6] This chapter examines the warfighting requirements for addressing terrorism and then does the same with respect to stabilization missions. It integrates current Canadian military capabilities in each of these areas and makes recommendations for the future.

MILITARY REQUIREMENTS
FOR WARFIGHTING OPERATIONS

Precision

The historical progression from the vast armies of the Napoleonic Revolution, to the more technologically sophisticated yet still large armies of the Cold War era, to smaller forces targeting smaller units (for example, missile batteries around Sarajevo) in the peace enforcement operations of the 1990s, has reached its logical conclusion in the post-9/11 era. Today military forces may be involved in targeting not a corps, a division, a battalion, or even a small military unit, but, in many cases, a specific individual. Just as the perpetrator of threats to North America has become more precise, the eradication of these threats has demanded greater precision in warfare. "Our opponents may be few in number, and highly mobile, presenting difficult and fleeting targets. They may be intermingled with a non-combatant population ... or they may be holed up in inaccessible locations ... in these circumstances, the accurate pin-pointing of targets, and the ability to strike hard with a high degree of precision, will all be important."[7]

Over the past ten years there has been a trend towards using more precision air power in military campaigns. In the war on terrorism in Afghanistan special operations forces on the ground and unmanned aerial vehicles flying overhead pinpointed coordinates for precision naval and air strikes against Taliban and Al Qaeda positions. In Iraq, precision firepower from a variety of American and British air and naval platforms similarly targeted and destroyed numerous specific regime-oriented objectives, including command-and-control sites, communications lines, and air defence installations. In Iraq and, especially, in Afghanistan unmanned aerial vehicles configured for combat missions also carried out precision strikes.

Land-based fighters are likely to be less useful in addressing threats abroad in the future. Although the Pentagon is pursuing plans to a create a network of small bases throughout the Middle East and central Asia,[8] finding a location close to the scene of a conflict from which to deploy a land-based tactical fighter aircraft will continue to be difficult. Recognizing this, the United States is concentrating its power-projection resources on assets that do not require a land base. It is purchasing a next-generation aircraft carrier, scaling back the land-based variant of the Joint Strike Fighter in favour of the carrier-based version, reducing the number of air force F-22 buys, and flying strategic bombers from the continental United States. The United States is also moving towards sea basing – having joint military forces operate from ships offshore rather than from land bases.[9]

Canada's CF-18 Hornets played a major precision air power role in the Kosovo crisis and could do so again in a similar crisis once command and control upgrades to the aircraft – including Link-16 data links and an onboard global positioning system device – are completed, in 2006. Since 1996 the CF-18s have been equipped with the capability to conduct precision bombing with laser-guided munitions. More recently, Canada's air force has evaluated a number of satellite-guided weapons for its fighter aircraft, including the enhanced Paveway 2 and Paveway 3 munitions, Joint Direct Attack Munition, and Joint Standoff Weapon, with a view to selection and eventual acquisition.[10] Canada has also signed on as an informed partner to America's Joint Strike Fighter program – a sensible move, given the associated industrial benefits and the need to keep its options open. But if Canada proceeds to acquire the land-based version of the Joint Strike Fighter for roles abroad, it could result in a capability that is not relevant to future overseas contingencies. Wear and tear on the CF-18 airframe dictate that the aircraft will have to be replaced by 2020, at the latest, but decisions on the follow-on aircraft should be guided more by renewed air defence requirements at home than by possible participation in strike operations abroad.

Support to Forces Ashore

Canada's precision-force capabilities should be concentrated in the maritime element. Since the end of the Cold War, Western air forces and navies have not confronted an enemy with technologically sophisticated forces at sea or in the air. As a result, the primary function of air forces and navies is to protect and deliver ground forces to a particular area and to support those forces with precision firepower.[11] While a case can be made that in some situations air power may be able fight a war on its own – the NATO operation in and around Kosovo in 1999 is probably the historical example that comes the closest – this is not the situation when it comes to naval forces. Today navies are expected to operate in the littoral regions in support of ground forces ashore, yet Canada's navy has no capability for projecting power ashore. In future its naval vessels will need to be equipped with the capability to carry out precision strikes against targets ashore for the purpose of protecting Canadian troops. The defence component of *Canada's International Policy Statement* highlights this precision force requirement,[12] while the chief of defence staff has proposed the acquisition of an amphibious assault ship for landing troops on shore.[13]

There is a growing interest among major naval powers in warships that have land attack and naval fire support as core mission capabilities.[14] One example of this is America's conversion of four

Trident nuclear submarines into land attack vessels equipped with a small crew complement and numerous land attack cruise missiles. In addition, all of America's fighter-based aircraft have been upgraded for land attack missions, and the naval version of the Joint Strike Fighter is being developed for this role. In the war on terrorism in Afghanistan and the conflict in Iraq, many precision strike missions were conducted from American and British submarines as well as American surface ships.

Advanced ISR and Command and Control

Striking hard with high degree of precision depends upon precise targeting information and the ability to disseminate it in near-real time. As the British Ministry of Defence points out, "Terrorist organisations are very difficult to identify, locate, quantify, monitor and target ... There is no magic solution to this problem. But it does reinforce the importance of maximising our ability to acquire, process and disseminate information."[15] Acquiring information demands advanced intelligence-gathering, surveillance, and reconnaissance (ISR) capabilities, while processing and disseminating information requires advanced command, control, communications, computing, and intelligence-processing (C4I) methods.

Advanced ISR can be achieved with a variety of platforms, including satellites and manned aircraft like America's Joint Surveillance Target Attack Radar System (JSTARS) aircraft and Britain's Airborne Stand-Off Radar aircraft. But the surveillance platform that has received the greatest attention in the post-9/11 era is the unmanned aerial vehicle (UAV). First used in the 1991 Gulf War, UAVs have become crucial to the ability of militaries to see over the next hill. The long-range Predator and the strategic Global Hawk UAVs figured prominently in the war on terrorism in Afghanistan. The medium-altitude Predator tracked individuals on the ground, while the high-altitude Global Hawk conducted extensive strategic surveillance and reconnaissance.

The combination of UAVs and advanced command, control, and communications assets enabled forces in Afghanistan to act on information in near-real time. UAVs provided an almost continuous flow of information to the air and naval platforms delivering precision munitions. By contrast, during the first Gulf War it took hours to get a UAV over a particular area and sometimes days to get the information to a commander. The Pentagon has dubbed this revolutionary development "persistent ISR." Advanced information-processing systems and software were used to gather, fuse, and analyze the information received, while advanced communications assets like tactical data links were used to rapidly disseminate information and instructions. The overall effect was to allow commanders to come close to controlling the battle from one moment to the next. Real-time information-sharing for situational awareness, and the translation of this information into rapid precision strike through advanced command and control technologies, is the essence of network-centric warfare.

Canada has no satellites for ISR, nor does it have a JSTARS equivalent, although it is participating in NATO's Air-Ground Surveillance (AGS) project, under which the alliance plans to acquire up to six AGS aircraft by 2013.[16] Its long-range patrol aircraft are being upgraded with a ground moving target indication capability, and the Canadian army acquired several tactical UAVs in the fall of 2003 to deploy to Afghanistan. But for advanced ISR Canada will need to invest more heavily in UAVs. These platforms have been used extensively in all recent conflicts, are highly relevant to stabilization missions, and could be useful in a homeland defence role. The CF has field tested a number of UAVs and has plans to purchase some for missions at home and abroad, but turning these plans into reality will be dependent on future funding.

Canada's advanced C4I capability includes a number of different systems. Under the Canadian Military Satellite Communications program, DND is paying the US military $250 million to add a payload onto America's advanced Extremely High Frequency (EHF) satellite system. This will give the CF its first dedicated military satellite communications capability by providing secure data and voice communications to its units around the world. The advanced EHF system is to have an initial operating capability in 2009; until then, the Canadian military will continue to rely on rental agreements with commercial satellites for long-range military communications.

As for the individual services, the Canadian navy's command and control systems are already fully interoperable with those of the US Navy, allowing Canadian ships to fit seamlessly into an American carrier battle group. The CF-18 upgrade program will make Canada's fighter aircraft interoperable with current American platforms; additional upgrades should only be made if they are relevant to the air defence role at home. And the army's Intelligence, Surveillance, Target Acquisition, and Reconnaissance (ISTAR) project is developing technology to link battlefield sensors from a variety of Canadian ground force platforms, now including UAVS,[17] as well as air and naval platforms. In future ISTAR will have to go further in two directions. First, it must take into account the need for Canadian platforms to receive information from, and transmit information to, American and other allied platforms. Second, given the growing role and relevance of stabilization operations, it must address the requirement for military forces to communicate with civilian organizations. Networked communications among services and allied militaries are crucial for high-intensity operations, but in stabilization missions it is necessary to couple military networks with civilian communications systems.

Special Operations Forces

In the post-9/11 era precision warfare has gone beyond air and sea power. The war on terrorism in Afghanistan demonstrated increasing precision in land warfare through the extensive use of special operations forces. "Special operations forces" can be defined as "specially organized, trained and equipped military and para-military forces that conduct ... operations to achieve military, political, economic or informational objectives by generally unconventional means in hostile, denied or politically sensitive areas."[18]

In the war on terrorism in Afghanistan special operations forces, including members of Canada's Joint Task Force 2 (JTF 2), called in air strikes from air and naval platforms, conducted operations to eradicate Al Qaeda and Taliban forces in caves, and provided support to indigenous land forces. These forces were also used extensively in Iraq in 2003 to ensure that Iraq did not fire Scud missiles at Israel, to interdict Iraqi supply lines to Syria, to mobilize the Kurds, to capture some northern towns, and to prevent Iraqi soldiers from destroying the nation's oil fields.[19] All told, some 6,000 special operations forces were deployed to Afghanistan in 2001–02, and even this large (by historical standards) figure was surpassed in Iraq in 2003, when 10,000 special operations forces were deployed in the war's first week.[20]

In the wake of the war in Afghanistan Western defence establishments have placed greater emphasis on special operations forces. The United States significantly increased the budget and forces assigned to its Special Operations Command and elevated its status. Rather than being just a force provider to other commands – as it had been since its creation in 1987 – US Special Operations Command now has the authority to plan and execute specific missions in the war on terror. Australia has created a new special operations force of some 1,800 highly trained troops, and their command will join Australia's[21] sea, land, and air commands as a fourth arm of defence. Britain is improving the capabilities of its special operations forces, primarily through better equipment rather than greater numbers, and Canada announced soon after 9/11 that it would double its JTF 2 from 300 to 600 people. The CF is also establishing a special operations group comprised of JTF 2, helicopters, and supporting land and maritime forces.[22] The increased utility of special operations forces in missions abroad, combined with their traditional and perhaps growing role in domestic counterterrorism, indicates that JTF 2 should be doubled again to between 1,000 and 1,200 troops.[23] Canada's new defence blueprint states the intention to enlarge JTF 2, but no specific figures are given.[24]

The growing role of special operations forces reflects not only the requirement for greater precision but also the realization that in some cases unconventional threats require unconventional responses. "The nature of the enemy, and the need for fast, efficient operations in hunting down and rooting out terrorist networks have all contributed to the need for an expanded role for Special Operations Forces."[25] Experts predict that the operations of special forces will be more closely integrated with those of conventional forces, and that conventional forces will increasingly find themselves in close combat situations that resemble special operations missions.[26] In the past, Canadian regular army units have been trained in special operations tactics, but, given warfare trends, it would be sensible to reverse recent decisions to forego this practice.[27] When it comes to JTF 2, it will be necessary to find an appropriate balance between overseas special forces capabilities and JTF 2's traditional domestic counterterrorism role.

Beyond special operations forces, precision land warfare also requires precision weaponry for both conventional and unconventional forces. The majority of ground force weapons are still area-fire weapons, which are incapable of attacking point targets, but the Afghanistan operation illustrated the need for precision strike artillery and mortars at the tactical level. The lack of such a capability in Afghanistan obliged ground forces to rely on precision firepower from above, in some cases leaving troops vulnerable to enemy fire.[28]

Mobility, Flexibility, and Speed on the Battlefield

The move from mass to precision is not the only change in the nature of warfare accelerating in the terrorist era. Another is the shift from opposing forces clashing on the front lines, seen throughout the industrial era, to non-linear, dispersed forces. In the post-9/11 world "there may be no clear 'front lines' separating opponents from our own forces or those of coalition partners."[29] Mobility, flexibility, and speed on the battlefield are therefore crucial in order to "fight enemies who may be difficult to pin down."[30] These characteristics are achieved through equipment and organizational changes. They create a large and growing role for helicopters in providing tactical mobility on the battlefield, they demand a deployment of highly lethal and survivable army platforms that are lighter and more manœuvrable, and they necessitate a restructuring of forces into smaller, more mobile units.

At first the spectre of Abrams and Challenger main battle tanks and Bradley and Warrior armoured fighting vehicles moving over the Iraqi desert during the 2003 conflict in Iraq undermined the notion that mobility, flexibility, and speed on the battlefield had trumped the large, heavy, linear forces developed during the Cold War. But the heavy platforms that were used, which happened to be in the American and British inventory, were adapted in the Iraqi conflict to the growing requirement for speed and mobility. Despite using heavy platforms, coalition planners sought to achieve military victory through velocity, not mass. Tanks and armoured fighting vehicles sped ahead and around obstacles in their drive to Baghdad, often leaving the logistics tail behind and open to ambush. This was a calculated risk taken by commanders who sought to maintain speed "by making the tip of the spear as supple, mobile, and flexible as possible."[31] As part of this strategy Apache ground attack helicopters assisted destroying tanks, vehicles, and other targets, while Black Hawk helicopters moved close-combat soldiers hundreds of miles inland to strike deep within enemy territory.

Within the next few years American and British heavy army platforms are set to be replaced with lighter systems that are just as lethal, and provide just as much force protection, as today's main battle tanks and armoured fighting vehicles. They include America's Future Combat System of vehicles and those of Britain's Future Rapid Effects System. The platforms within each of these families of vehicles – the Future Combat System, for example, is to include sixteen to twenty different vehicles – will be far more mobile on the battlefield than present-day systems. A number of advanced technologies will contribute to their increased mobility, but the most important features are their decreased weight (from a Cold War average of seventy tons to a stated ceiling of twenty tons) and the fact that they are to be wheeled, rather than tracked, platforms.

In organizational terms, the ground force that fought the 2003 Iraqi war was not that much different from the one deployed to the 1991 Gulf War. The forces were parcelled out, as they were in first Gulf War, into corps, divisions, and brigades (marine expeditionary forces, divisions, and brigades in the case of the marines). Nonetheless, the conflict hinted at changes to come, and indications are that there are more dramatic developments ahead. The total number of American and British forces deployed in and around Iraq in 2003 was less than half that of the coalition force deployed to carry out the 1991 Gulf War's objectives. Moreover, future warfighting plans are to be based not only on a smaller overall force size (as compared to Cold War levels), but also on smaller units within that force.

The central ground force unit of the future is likely to be a brigade, rather than a corps or even a division. The transformation to smaller, more mobile units is already being reflected in America's new Stryker Brigade Combat Teams, the first of which was deployed to Iraq at the end of 2003. These 3,600-soldier units are being equipped with the Stryker Light Armoured Vehicle, a highly mobile eight-wheeled platform that can travel one hundred kilometres an hour, weighs just nineteen tons, and is equipped with a 105-millimetre gun. Early evidence suggests that the vehicle is providing just the sort of operational agility and capability that the US Army wants.[32] The Stryker Mobile Gun System has been the subject of considerable criticism, both in the United States and Canada, for being vulnerable to rocket-propelled grenades and not offering sufficient protection to the soldiers that operate it. But the Stryker was never intended for front-line combat. This role will be reserved for the Future Combat System and, if the opportunity presents itself, Canada should consider becoming an informed partner in that program.

America's new light armoured brigades are to be part of the most significant reorganization of US ground forces since the end of the Cold War. The current US Army leadership plans to restructure the army's thirty-three brigades into forty-eight smaller, more versatile units for overseas deployment. These brigades are to be more modular, in that personnel will be rotated unit by unit rather than individually, allowing companies and battalions to be mixed and matched according to the requirements of the mission.[33] They are also to be more self-sustaining and have more combat power than current brigades, enabling the Pentagon to respond to smaller-scale contingencies by deploying a brigade of up to 5,000 soldiers instead of a much larger division of 20,000 soldiers.

After the release of the 1999 US Army vision statement *Soldiers on Point for the Nation: Persuasive in Peace, Invincible in War*, Strykers were billed as part of America's "interim" force, referring to a middle step between "legacy forces," armed with tanks, and a "future force," featuring the Future Combat System. But Stryker brigades are no longer expected to be an interim step. Rather, three types of US Army brigades are expected to coexist: heavy brigades, armed with tanks and Bradley fighting vehicles until the Future Combat System comes into production; medium brigades, armed with motorized infantrymen (the Stryker brigades); and airborne brigades, armed with Apache helicopters and paratroopers.[34]

The Canadian army is taking a number of steps in response to the requirement for more rapidly deployable ground forces. In 2002 it began a process of reconfiguring its three brigade groups to create a medium-weight, information-age land force. In accordance with the army strategy released that year, all armoured forces have been amalgamated in the brigade group in Edmonton, making this Canada's only heavy brigade. The tanks that make up the brigade will be replaced with the Mobile Gun System, transforming it into a medium-weight brigade. The other two brigade groups have become lightweight strike forces equipped with the light armoured vehicle (LAV III) and Coyote reconnaissance vehicles that have proven so valuable in overseas contingencies.

Canada's decision to purchase the Stryker Mobile Gun System is a sensible one. Despite the reduced protection it offers combat troops, the system's substantial firepower coupled with high mobility fits well with many of the situations military forces are likely to find themselves in when battling international terrorism. Unlike tanks, Strykers are well-suited for city engagements and urban warfare.[35] They are also likely to play a significant role in providing security for a growing number of stabilization missions. Canada's acquisition of the Mobile Gun System, combined with the fact that Canada's army is organized around brigade groups, will make this army interoperable with that of the United States. But the army will remain highly limited in its tactical mobility. Canada has no battlefield helicopter; with no armament the Griffon helicopter cannot be considered a combat platform and is ill-suited to even medium-intensity operations. The result has been that in operations like the war on terrorism in Afghanistan, CF members have been totally reliant on the US military for air mobility in theatre. The February 2005 federal budget provided $12.8 billion in increased funding to the Canadian military over five years, most of which is allocated towards the end of that period. Some of this money has been earmarked for purchasing twelve to eighteen troop transport helicopters.

Rapid Deployability into Theatre

Many of the changes in equipment and organizational structure necessary to create a highly mobile force for a non-linear battlefield are consistent with a further warfighting requirement for addressing terrorism: rapid deployability to the area of operations. Operations in Afghanistan, for example, "made apparent the need to be able to deploy and redeploy ground forces rapidly into theatre."[36] For increased deployability units are being equipped with precision firepower, thus reducing the weight of ammunition they must carry. They are also being furnished with lighter, air-transportable equipment, like the Stryker, which can fit on a C-130 transport plane. Weight and size limitations figure centrally in development plans for both the Future Combat System and the Future Rapid Effects System so that they will also be air-transportable. And the units themselves are being made smaller and more modular. All this is part of a drive to make armies "lighter and more deployable for the global war on terror."[37]

But rapid deployability is ultimately dependent on the existence of strategic lift, including airlift and sealift. Many countries are focusing on acquiring the necessary air force platforms to make their forces expeditionary. America has over a hundred C-17 Globemaster strategic transport aircraft, with plans to build more, while Britain is purchasing five of these aircraft. Several European countries are part of the program to develop and acquire the AM-400 Future Large Aircraft, due for delivery by the end of the decade, while NATO as an organization is also examining the possibility of leasing Ukrainian Antonov strategic airlift aircraft.

Canada has no strategic airlift capability to rapidly deploy its ground forces and their equipment to trouble spots around the world. When it comes to missions like Afghanistan, for example, Canada is dependent on the US to get its forces and equipment into theatre. Currently, the backbone of Canada's military airlift is its Hercules C-130 aircraft, but their size, range, and speed make them more of a tactical than a strategic transport platform. Moreover, because these aircraft are old, overworked, and often under repair, less than half the fleet is available on any given day. Canada is part of NATO's strategic lift initiative, but funding disputes make it unclear whether it will actually go forward.

At the same time, Canada has no dedicated naval transport ships for moving equipment overseas and must rent commercial vessels for this purpose or transport its troops on allied vessels. This shortfall in sealift is in the early stages of being partially rectified. The CF has received funding approval for three Joint Support Ships, which will combine capabilities for fleet replenishment at sea, sealift for army units, and a joint force headquarters for command and control of units on shore. Once delivered, at the beginning of the next decade, the ships will be able to transport the equivalent of 300 light army trucks.[38] Although this is welcome news, military experts point out that the acquisition will still only provide a limited sealift capability. The Joint Support Ship is "an extremely valuable and absolutely essential addition to the Canadian Forces' capability. However, it does not create an expeditionary capability."[39] To transport the troops and equipment for a battalion group (approximately 1,000 personnel) – the most common unit that Canada deploys overseas – would require all three Joint Support Ships.

Jointness

To effectively combat threats in today's security environment, land, sea, and air forces have become increasingly interdependent in their operations. This is because many of the warfighting attributes central to combatting terrorism – like speed and flexibility on a non-linear battlefield and greater lethality with less mass – require that ground forces be able to call in precision air and naval power. The Pentagon has captured this synergy in a new doctrine of "rapid decisive operations," which centres on the close integration of air power, special forces, and mobile ground formations.[40]

Recent conflicts have demonstrated a growing degree of jointness among military services. In the war on terrorism in Afghanistan there was extraordinary synchronization between land and air power, including naval air power. Special operations forces on horseback provided target information to the ships, bombers, and fighter aircraft firing precision weapons, dramatically enhancing their accuracy and effectiveness. The US special operations forces themselves were drawn from the navy, army, and air force, and they operated in seamless co-operation. In Iraq, army Black Hawk helicopters called in close air strikes from Royal Navy Harrier fighter jets, US Air Force A-10 Warthog tank busters, and US Navy F-18s.[41] Strategic bombers provided close air support to ground forces, while heavy armour supported special operations forces.[42] Special forces also called in air strikes against critical regime targets.

While the concept of air-land coordination in battle has been around for almost as long as the airplane, the Iraqi conflict saw an unprecedented partnership between air power and ground manœuvre. General Richard Myers, chairman of the Joint Chiefs of Staff, attributed the efficient progress of the war to a vastly improved picture of the battlefield and a new willingness on the part of commanders to use the most appropriate capabilities available, regardless of which service was providing them.[43] In many cases lower-level army commanders did not know whether precision firepower was coming from the air force, navy, or marines.

Interdiction Operations

In the contemporary security environment naval forces need to be able to interdict ships that might be carrying terrorists and their weapons and to conduct counter-mining operations close to shore. Interdiction operations, such as those carried out by the Canadian navy in the Arabian Sea from 2001 to 2003 (Operation Apollo), make a tangible contribution to international security. Future operations of this nature are likely to be carried out under the Proliferation Security Initiative, launched by the United States in 2003. Prompted by the case of the *Sosan*, a North Korean ship that was discovered carrying Scud missiles to Yemen in December 2002, the initiative aims to create a multilateral setting for stopping worldwide shipments of weapons of mass destruction by allowing the United States and its allies to search a plane or ship suspected of carrying deadly cargo and seize illegal weapons, even if the plane or ship is not in the member country's airspace or territorial waters. Canada joined the initiative early in 2004. Although some countries, like Russia and China, have questioned its legality, Canada has argued that the legal basis can be found in the Nuclear Non-proliferation Treaty and other international agreements.[44] The initiative responds to the reality that the spread of nuclear, chemical, and biological weapons "is not a subset of the war on terrorism but a huge danger in its own right."[45]

The US Navy is in the process of developing a littoral combat ship for maritime interdiction operations. Scheduled to be ready by the end of the decade, the ship will be designed to operate in heavily contested waters near the shore to counter mines, submarines, and fast attack boats.[46] But currently the naval platform best suited to the "global coast guard role" of interdiction operations is frigates.[47] For this reason, as well as for the interdiction role it will play in waters off North America (see chapter 5), Canada's fleet of Halifax-Class Multi-role Patrol Frigates must be upgraded. Although the ships are among the navy's most modern, they are reaching the halfway point in their design life and will soon need a refit. Moreover, maritime surveillance and control – whether off the shores of North America or in the Arabian Sea – is best conducted with a naval task group (see chapter 5), including a command and control destroyer. For this reason, Canada's ageing Iroquois-class destroyers, which date to 1970, need to be replaced. Early indications are that the navy will seek a new class of ship that combines the capabilities of the destroyers and the frigates.[48] Finally, Canada's ships sometimes sit in dry dock for lack of personnel; the Canadian navy needs about 2,000 additional people just to man its current vessels,[49] and it would need even more should Canada decide to purchase an amphibious ship.

The navy's task groups cannot operate independently without its supply ships – the Auxiliary Oil Replenishment ships, which are also aging, and very close to the end of their operational life. Canada's new Joint Support Ships, which are primarily intended for fleet replenishment, will therefore be central to the navy's ability to contribute to interdiction operations. But some observers and experts have begun to question the advisability of putting so many capabilities on one ship. Although Joint Support Ships would be useful in inserting troops and equipment into benign environments, a vessel carrying lots of people and lots of fuel would make an attractive enemy target.[50] Moreover, one can easily envisage a scenario in which the navy needs refuelling capabilities in one part of the world, while the army needs sealift and offshore command and control in an entirely different region.[51]

MILITARY REQUIREMENTS
FOR STABILIZATION OPERATIONS

Warfighting is only one role of military forces abroad in the post-9/11 security environment – and not the most likely. Stabilization and reconstruction missions to rebuild a country in the wake of a warfighting operation, prevent a slide into warfare, or stabilize and restore order to a failed or failing state will be far more commonplace. Failed states create an environment in which terrorists can establish a base of operations to inflict harm on North America. Countries such as Afghanistan, where terrorists have been routed out, pose a security threat to the Western world until they have been reconstructed and stabilized. Peace-building in the 1990s was primarily seen as a humanitarian undertaking that, while worthy, was not directly related to the security of North America. The events of 11 September 2001 profoundly altered this view, demonstrating that North America is not immune to troubles afflicting other parts of the world, and indicating that stabilization and reconstruction missions, no less than those of warfighting, can be central to North American security and defence. Canada has stated its continued intention to participate in military missions against terrorist networks and the states that harbour them.[52] But, given the prevalence of failed and failing states and their direct impact, in certain cases, on Canadian security, its decision to focus CF efforts abroad on stabilization and reconstruction missions is an appropriate one.

As is the case with find-and-strike operations, stabilization operations demand a military force with a particular set of characteristics. Many of these characteristics are consistent with those identified as essential to effective warfighting in the future. Advanced intelligence, surveillance, and reconnaissance capabilities are crucial for gaining a complete picture of circumstances throughout the area that military forces are attempting to stabilize. This means that the acquisition of unmanned aerial vehicles, for example, is equally an investment in stabilization capability and in combat strength. UAVs are seen to be particularly useful in overcoming the challenges of concealment associated with the urban environment.[53]

Similarly, advanced command and control capabilities are required to link the many military and civilian forces engaged in a stabilization task. Therefore, systems that are designed to enable the rapid transmission of information and commands between platforms and forces in wartime also contribute to stabilization capability. Indeed, the challenges here may be even greater than in warfighting: networked communications among services and allied militaries are crucial for combat operations, but in stabilization missions is it necessary to go a step further and couple the military network with civilian communications systems.

The smaller, more mobile modular units discussed in terms of warfighting are also highly relevant for stabilization missions in which troops need to navigate narrow, winding roads and respond rapidly to isolated circumstances that are ultimately non-linear in nature. Moreover, these forces need a certain degree of combat capability. In many cases stabilization forces face a precarious internal security situation; they must have combat platforms that can both protect them and allow a show of force, if necessary. Special operations forces, too, are well suited to carrying out important aspects of a stabilization and reconstruction mission, such as ensuring the security of critical infrastructures. Finally, force deployability and access to strategic airlift and sealift capabilities are just as relevant to stabilization as warfighting missions, since, ultimately, both tasks take place far from North American shores.

That said, certain attributes of a warfighting force have limited application to stabilization operations. Air- and sea-launched precision munitions, for example, and all their associated platforms, may be of little value in this phase of a conflict. In addition, some characteristics of a stabilization mission are significantly different from those of warfighting.

Critical Mass

Perhaps the greatest distinction between requirements of warfighting and those of stabilization missions is the overall size of the force. Warfighting calls for smaller units to move rapidly over the battlefield using advanced technology to ensure that they are just as lethal as yesterday's larger forces. Comparing the Cold War and post-9/11 eras, new technologies have already brought about a roughly two-thirds reduction in the number of forces required for warfighting: a contemporary brigade can command as much ground as a Cold War division.[54] Although technology can make a difference, the principle of substituting technology for troops is a less relevant option in stabilization missions than in warfighting. Nation-building demands a certain critical mass of people – not larger units, but more units, and thus a larger overall force size. Tellingly, in Iraq in 2003 the United States needed nine brigades to fight the war, but twelve brigades to secure the peace.[55]

Combat Support and Combat Service Support

Another distinction between warfighting and stabilization missions is in the balance of units required. Generally speaking, stabilization missions call for more combat support (signals, combat engineers, military police) personnel and more combat service support (transport, supply, administration, psychological operations, civil-military affairs, medical, water purification) personnel than do warfighting operations. Traditionally, brigades have been designed with three battalions of combat soldiers and roughly one battalion of combat support and combat service support units. At the division level, this 3:1 ratio translates into roughly nine battalions of combat forces and three of support elements. The combat support and combat service support units are deployed over and over again in response to stabilization mission requirements, with the result that some – but not all – of the army experiences a very high degree of operational tempo. To rectify this problem, and, in effect, to spread the workload around, the Pentagon has begun to look at creating military forces specifically for stabilization operations.[56]

A report prepared by the National Defense University for the Pentagon's influential Office of Force Transformation has recommended that the US field one or two "stabilization and reconstruction" divisions. These would number about 15,000 soldiers each and be dedicated to preventative or post-conflict measures to build or rebuild a society.[57] Each division would include a mix of combat and combat support/service support personnel better suited to the stabilization and reconstruction mission than traditional combat divisions. The core combat component would consist of one Stryker Brigade (three battalions). The remainder of the division would be made up of combat service and service support battalions, including military police, civil affairs, construction engineers, medical personnel, psychological operations, and communications. In essence, the traditional 3:1 ratio of combat to combat support units would be more than reversed in a stabilization and reconstruction division. Indications are that the ability to carry out post-conflict stability operations will figure prominently in America's 2006 *Quadrennial Defense Review.*[58]

Canada should look closely at US thinking on the creation of stabilization and reconstruction divisions. A Canadian adaptation might involve arming brigades with the Mobile Gun System and significantly increasing the size of brigade groups to include many more units of combat support and combat service support forces. Canada could aim to bring the traditional 3:1 ratio of combat to combat support/combat service support units up to an even ratio of 3:3 (1:1), or a minimum increase of close to 5,000 troops in the brigade groups alone. In today's security environment, at home and abroad, the CF is simply not large enough, and people, as much as new equipment, need to be the focus of Canada's future defence investments.

Technologies Unique to Peace-Building

A final key distinction between warfighting and stabilization operations concerns necessary technologies and weapons for stabilization operations. The military role in a stabilization operation will in some ways be similar to a domestic military operation in aid of the civil power. Whereas non-lethal weapons do not figure in warfighting calculations, they would be very useful in stabilization missions. Forces will need technologies designed to counter guerrilla and sniper fire, engage in crowd control, conduct border and perimeter security, and ensure the safe transportation of passengers. More traditional post-conflict activities will also be necessary, such as mine detection and removal, while increased intelligence from local sources to detect, track, and ultimately neutralize hostile individuals such as suicide bombers will be imperative.[59]

CONCLUSION

In the terrorist era Canadian security will require the CF to be able to undertake both warfighting and stabilization missions. A number of force attributes stand out as relevant to both types of mission, including unmanned aerial vehicles, advanced command and control systems, mobile and deployable forces, and strategic airlift and sealift. If one takes into account warfighting and stabilization force attributes that are also relevant to homeland defence missions, then equipment and personnel priorities become even clearer. UAVs will need to keep watch along Canada's vast shorelines, strategic airlift will be required to get disaster response forces and their equipment across the country, and Canada's navy will have to carry out interdiction operations off North American shores as well as foreign shores. A small warfighting force can form the nucleus of a larger stabilization force, but increased force size also responds to homeland requirements for aid of the civil power. At one time it was possible to argue that Canada's best response to the post–Cold War security environment was to focus on those force attributes cross-suited to warfighting and peace support operations. In the post-9/11 security environment it is imperative to add homeland defence considerations to the equation.

8

Canadian Security and Defence in the Terrorist Era

"Getting the right balance between domestic and international security concerns," argues Canada's first national security policy, "will be an important consideration in determining the roles and force structure of the Canadian Forces."[1] Although this is true, the real issue is much broader in scope. Finding the right balance between measures at home to defend against the threat and operations abroad to combat it before it can reach Canada's shores is central to whether the Canadian government can carry out its ultimate responsibility of guaranteeing the security of its citizens.

One of the most important questions for Canada and the United States to address is whether it is more effective to defend North America by taking homeland security and defence measures against terrorism or by seeking out and destroying international terrorism overseas. The answer will not be absolute – both offensive and defensive measures will inevitably be required. Rather, the task is to find the most appropriate balance. If a state has one dollar to spend on national security, roughly what proportion of that dollar should be spent on defensive measures and forces at home and what proportion on offensive forces for operations abroad? Although this is a difficult question to answer, it may be possible to formulate at least an approximate answer based on the responses to several sets of sub-questions.

FACTORS IN THE BALANCE

The Nature of the Threat

The first set of sub-questions centres on the nature of the threat. What are the primary threats to North America today? How easy/

difficult is it to detect these threats? What would be today's equivalent of looking for armies massing? The primary threat to North America today is international terrorism, and specifically individuals and networks of individuals operating in terror cells dispersed around the globe, including within North America. To secure the safety of citizens, today's governments are not on the lookout for military formations, as they would have been in the past, "but for a lone, unknown person in a visa line."[2]

This is an exceedingly difficult threat to detect. "For a state to seek out individuals and networks," points out one scholar, "is like seeking the needle of criminal activity in the haystack of an increasingly complex society."[3] Indeed, it is hard for a law enforcement or internal security agency to detect the activities of small numbers of people, even if they are operating illegally. According to US law enforcement experts, the core challenge is the initial detection of a dangerous group – it is enormously difficult. Once this is done, however, there is a range of tools the United States and Canada can use to keep tabs on potentially dangerous individuals.[4]

Finding the needle in the haystack is doubly hard today because the identity of the needle keeps changing – and moving. "The terrorists that intelligence must uncover are not inert objects; they are living, conniving strategists."[5] One element of the new terrorism is a trend towards terrorist activity among individuals with no previous record of terrorist involvement, and therefore without a data bank entry against which they can be verified. This problem of fresh faces makes it hard to adopt a policy of denying potential terrorists entry to North America. That said, it might be possible to narrow the field by focusing on detecting behaviour in which only members of terrorist groups are likely to engage. The best-known example of such behaviour, now almost a cliché, is taking flying lessons but expressing a lack of interest in learning landing or takeoff procedures. Other examples include renting crop-dusters with no crops to dust, or acquiring fermenting equipment suitable only for brewing beer or producing anthrax.[6]

Today's equivalent of looking for armies massing is picking up increased "chatter" pertaining to a planned terrorist attack – particularly, specific threat information from electronic eavesdropping/communications intercepts and interrogations of detained prisoners.[7]

Chatter from intercepted phone calls and e-mails, for example, raised security concerns in the months prior to the 2004 US federal elections.[8] But now that terrorists have become wise to the pitfalls of using cellphones, much current intelligence on possible attacks comes from interviews with captured Al Qaeda members.[9]

In the contemporary environment, more so than in any previous period, there is an absolute premium on intelligence information. Whereas at one time governments might have built fortresses or dug trenches or followed trends in the policies of a state, today the first line of defence is to develop a robust intelligence network that can warn the government of an attack so that it can be stopped before it is launched.[10] But achieving this is far from assured. The ambiguity of partial warnings and the ability of terrorists to overcome obstacles and manipulate information, not to mention the language barriers and the near impossibility of penetrating small, disciplined organizations with alien cultures like Al Qaeda, means that no system can be foolproof. "The awful truth," says one intelligence expert, "is that even the best intelligence systems will have big failures."[11]

In some ways the difficulty-of-detection issue is less pronounced abroad. Although individual Al Qaeda members proved hard to detect within the US, the mass of the Al Qaeda organization and the general location of its base of operations, Afghanistan, was easily discovered. This was the only place in the world where the threat did not manifest itself as a network of small terrorist cells, but rather as a significant organization that operated with the consent and support of the government. In this respect another contemporary form of looking for armies massing at the border may be identifying weak states unable to control their territories. In the future terrorist activity is unlikely to be overtly condoned, as it was in Afghanistan; instead, it will be facilitated by the inability of the host country to control the activity within its borders. In either case terrorist activity is likely to be somewhat more visible in such countries than it is in North America.

US intelligence agencies appear quite adept at identifying the failed states most likely to harbour terrorists and therefore pose a security threat to North America. The United States is focusing on five states in northeastern Africa – Somalia, Sudan, Eritrea, Ethiopia, and Djibouti – as well as on Yemen, using military training, humanitarian aid, and intelligence operations to ensure that these countries do not become the next Afghanistan.[12] There are real concerns that Sudan, especially, could become the next basing and breeding ground for international terrorism.[13] Given scarce resources, time, and energy, it is necessary to identify a clear set of high-priority countries.[14] Decisions as to which states to focus attention upon should be based on factors like the need to avert terrorists from establishing a base of operations.[15]

But, while it is important to focus on failed states, the fact is that an international terrorist organization like Al Qaeda has numerous small cells in dozens of countries, only a handful of which are failed states. The commuter-train bombings in Madrid well illustrate that "terrorists are living and operating within jurisdictions of US allies and do not need to receive aid and comfort from rogue states."[16]

Geography

A second set of sub-questions centres on geography, one of the two traditional factors in calculating the offence-defence balance. What is the general geographic situation of the state concerned? How have global economic trends, new technologies, and attributes of the threat impacted the geographic advantage? With oceans on the east and west and friendly continental neighbours to the south, Canada and the United States have, for the better part of two centuries – since they overcame their own differences – enjoyed a geography that largely protects them from the outside world. But since World War II increasing globalization has chipped away the geographic advantage of living in North America. Every year millions of passengers, airplanes, and ships arrive at North American airports and seaports. Millions more people, trucks, cars, and railway cars traverse the Canada-US border.[17] Advances in technology, notably the airplane, have made it possible for individuals around the world to reach North America within several hours. Globalization has opened North America to the benefits of a global trading environment, but it has also made the continent vulnerable to international terrorism.

Advances in technology have also made it possible to target North America without setting foot on, or indeed coming anywhere near, North American soil. The overwhelming dependence of modern societies on the smooth functioning of computer systems, combined with the interconnectedness of such systems around the world, makes computer systems an attractive target for computer-savvy terrorists. Historically, in order to attack a state an adversary had to physically make its way to that state – or at least develop accurate long-range weapons. But geography is no barrier to terrorists choosing to target a nation's critical information infrastructure. Today it is possible for an enemy to wreak havoc on North America without ever leaving home.

Another change in the geographic element of the offence/defence calculation is that today the greatest threat to a state may not be at its borders but within its borders. The terrorist attacks of 11 September 2001 were a tragic demonstration that the enemy at the gate may already be inside the gate. Prior to the 1990s terrorism was considered an evil that resided far from North America.[18] The 1993 attack on the World Trade Center and the 1995 Oklahoma City bombing shook this perception, but not until 9/11 was it clear that geographic locations traditionally defined as "rear area," such as the US homeland, could no longer be so categorized.[19] The type of terrorism that the Al Qaeda network espouses transcends national boundaries.[20]

Again, this situation represents a marked shift from previous historical periods, in which states always looked to their borders and beyond to identify potential threats to their citizens. Today defence is difficult because the range of attractive targets in North America is vast – there are far too many to actively defend. Certainly, it is possible to increase security at the most obvious targets, like government buildings and nuclear power plants. But it is physically impossible to cover all potentialities. Generally speaking, "those charged with the security of the United States [and Canada] must guess. They have to choose the targets they most want to protect, and also choose the targets that may be most attractive to terrorists."[21]

Civilian Technologies

A third set of sub-questions that must be addressed in trying to ascertain the offence/defence balance concerns civilian technologies. What advances have been made in civilian technologies for detecting/addressing contemporary threats to North America? Can current technologies tackle the huge task of monitoring transborder activity by sea, land, and air?

Since 9/11 the United States and Canada have implemented an enormous array of technologies to detect the terrorist threat and increase the security of the continent. Just a few examples include a sensor network in major cities designed to detect a biological weapons attack; Visitor and Immigrant Status Indicator Technology, which tracks visitors entering and leaving the United States; the NEXUS system of high-tech border clearance cards; the VACIS gamma ray system for searching trucks, passenger vehicles, and shipping containers for illegal items; radiation detectors to scan trucks and cars for radiation emissions and so-called dirty bombs; high-tech video surveillance systems along the border; an automatic identification system to analyze ship manifests and identify high-risk cargo containers before ships reach North American waters; and well-established but ever-advancing technologies for intercepting and processing billions of satellite-transmitted e-mails, faxes, and telephone conversations every day.

Clearly, progress in homeland security technologies has been significant. Although the magnitude of the task of monitoring goods and people entering the United States and Canada is mammoth, preliminary indications are that technological advances may, in the medium term, be largely up to the challenge. In at least one area – screening cargo containers that enter Canadian ports – projections suggest that what some would consider a robust screening process could be in place within the next few years. Indeed, it is probable that "technology – biometrics, data-mining, superfast data-processing, and ubiquitous video-surveillance – will move [the] needle-in-the-haystack problem into the just-possible category."[22] Experts have cited better security everywhere, "from airports to ballparks to nuclear plants," as well as dramatically improved intelligence-gathering at home and abroad, to explain why no repeat terrorist attacks were launched in the years immediately following 9/11.[23] This level of vigilance must be maintained even as that date recedes in time.

Military Technologies

Finally, the other factor traditionally used to calculate the offence/ defence balance, military technology, needs to be taken into account when examining how best to respond to the contemporary security environment. What is the character of advances in military technology? How applicable are they to deterring threats, striking terrorist organizations abroad, and defending the homeland?

Advances in military technologies centre on the increased precision, mobility, and long-range striking power of modern military forces. These attributes are often cited as contributing to the ability of the United States to deter rogue states or state sponsors of terrorism. America's ability to destroy a hostile nation's launch sites, storage sites, and production facilities with conventionally armed precision weapons, it is argued, would make a direct nuclear attack or nuclear extortion against an American ally very unlikely.[24] Moreover, force projection, or the ability to rapidly deploy military forces abroad, plays a key role in deterring regional challenges to US interests and allies, particularly considering the ongoing drawdown of America's military forces stationed overseas.[25] Should deterrence break down, the same military attributes upon which deterrence policies are based – rapid force projection overseas – would be effective in conducting the warfighting effort.

New military technologies and the accompanying doctrinal changes in Western forces are also relevant to some degree to directly targeting the international terrorist threat to North America in overseas settings. To take the offensive, the United States and its allies need to exploit intelligence on the existence and location of terrorist cells, supplementing general ideas about locations with specific intelligence – especially from tactical unmanned aircraft – on the precise coordinates of terrorist camps or clandestine units in hiding. Special operations forces are especially suited to the counterterrorist mission, as are the smaller, more mobile, yet highly lethal ground force units being developed by many Western armies. Nonetheless, conducting warfighting efforts against terrorists abroad will be a challenge. Terrorist groups are increasingly amorphous and more likely to use evolving information technologies and to rely on less traditional organizational structures, thus making it much harder to find targets to attack militarily.[26] "Targeting terrorism at its source is an appealing notion," notes one homeland security expert. "Unfortunately the enemy is not cooperating. There is no central front on which al Qaeda can be cornered and destroyed."[27]

If warfighting against terrorism will be difficult, deterrence will be a near impossibility. New military technology is less likely to be effective in changing the behaviour of a non-state actor than it is in addressing rogue states and state sponsors of terrorism, which occupy a piece of land. Moreover, the concept of deterrence fundamentally rests on a cost-benefit analysis, and it is very difficult to raise the costs of terrorism significantly, "since terrorists only need a few successes on the margins to make a political point."[28] Cost-benefit analyses are further complicated by the fact that terrorist groups might believe that an attack could not be traced back to them, or because its members might be seeking to die for their cause. The challenges of warfighting and deterrence in the contemporary environment have led even long-standing advocates of increased military expeditionary capabilities to argue in favour of placing a new priority on defensive capabilities to address the terrorist threat.[29]

Meanwhile, there have been some significant advances in homeland defence technologies, with promises of more to come. Most notable is the High Frequency Surface Wave Radar technology, which Canada has developed, and future space-based surveillance technologies, like America's space-based radar system. But challenges remain, particularly in the area of ballistic missile defence technology and defences against cruise missiles. "Even if the current NMD system eventually demonstrated a 90 percent rate of technical effectiveness [during testing]," a former (technology-minded) US secretary of defence has argued, "it is reasonable to question whether it could ever come close to that under operational conditions."[30] Moreover, an operationally effective BMD system would provide almost no protection against the more likely threat of a ship-launched cruise missile or a covert delivery achieved by smuggling or other means. Exploring technologies to address the cruise missile threat has not been a US priority, and specific requirements are only now being studied.

ASSESSING THE BALANCE

Examining some key factors in determining whether threats to North America can best be addressed by focusing on defensive measures at home or offensive measures abroad produces a mixed picture. The nature of the threat is such that it is an exceedingly difficult one to detect, both at home and abroad. Detection is dependent on picking up chatter – now possible due to technological advances – as well as on increased human intelligence, but no intelligence network can ever be foolproof. The advantages and pitfalls of intelligence figure equally in terms of the offence and the defence, since enhanced intelligence capabilities are necessary for both.[31] One area where the nature of the threat points to an overseas, offensive posture is in the rebuilding of failed states that clearly pose a security risk to North America.

Globalization, modern technologies, and the existence of internal threats have largely erased North America's historical defensive geographic advantage. But advances in civilian technologies are beginning to cancel out this loss, moving the enormous task of defending North America into the realm of the just possible. As for weapons and military technology, offence and defence appear to have equal weight. Advanced military technologies and the accompanying doctrinal changes make it possible to target terrorists abroad with military force, yet this is still an extraordinarily difficult task. Moreover, the traditional approach of using military force to deter the threat abroad is all but precluded. Meanwhile, important strides have been made in homeland defence technologies, or are on the horizon, but challenges remain in areas like ballistic and cruise missile defence.

This assessment reveals that the United States and Canada should give roughly equal weight to homeland security and defence measures and measures to defend the homeland abroad. To follow this prescription would be to depart from historical policy trends on both sides of the border. The nature of the threat during the Cold War was such that Canada and the United States placed much greater emphasis on measures abroad to provide security at home. "The basic premise," maintained a former US defence secretary, "is that unless we are prepared to defend parts of the world other than the North American continent, we will soon have nothing more than North America to defend."[32] This approach made sense, given the nature of the threat at the time. The predominance of intrastate conflict in areas around the world during the 1990s also supported a predominantly overseas approach.

Today the idea that the best defence is a good offence continues to inform US security policy. The mantra is stated explicitly in the September 2002 *National Security Strategy of the United States*, and its essence has been repeated in numerous presidential speeches. "The energetic defence of our nations is an important duty,"

President Bush declared on a state visit to Canada late in 2004. "Yet defence alone is not a sufficient strategy ... There is only one way to deal with enemies who plot in secret and set out to murder the innocent ... We must take the fight to them."[33] The notion of creating security at home by addressing threats abroad was also expressed in Canada in the early years after 9/11,[34] but this has begun to change. Officials note that while there is a need to deal with threats far from Canada, it is also clear that Canada is no longer isolated from threats and must increase its focus on its air and maritime approaches, including the Arctic.[35] "There is no home front," Prime Minister Martin declared in a speech to CF members in 2004. "The conflict is not 'over there.'"[36] Recent policy documents state explicitly that a greater emphasis needs to be placed on the defence of Canada and North America than in the past.[37] Driven by a combination of the nature of the threat, geography, and advances in military and civilian technology, this is a marked change in approach, and it needs to be made if governments in North America are to fulfill their primary responsibility of guaranteeing the security of citizens. The bigger challenge now will be to ensure that this new emphasis makes its way into future military capital-acquisition decisions.

CONCLUSION

Finding the most appropriate balance between taking security and defence measures at home and using the military instrument abroad goes a long way towards determining the essential components of Canada's national security strategy. But it is still only part of the answer. Indeed, no national security strategy will be complete if it does not account for the fourth quadrant – the more comprehensive, largely civilian-led efforts overseas to address threats to Canadian security. One idea being pursued by Canada's Department of Foreign Affairs is taking a 3-D approach to creating a safer world. This would involve integrating defence, diplomacy, and development to bring stability to areas of the world that are most prone to becoming safe havens for terrorist organizations. The thinking behind this is that for Canada's activities abroad to be effective, they must be part of a coordinated diplomatic, military, and foreign aid response. Perhaps the best representation of this approach is the provincial reconstruction teams that have been established in Afghanistan – teams of fifty to one hundred civilian and military specialists, including combat engineers and workers from non-governmental aid organizations, protected by infantry.

More broadly, a key and perhaps unstated objective of Canada's national security strategy must be to increase Canada's credibility and influence with the United States. This is important because it would put Canada in a position to encourage the United States to adopt patterns of behaviour that would ultimately increase Canadian security. At the strategic level there are various ways of organizing the international system, aside from the unlikely option of creating a world government. Some countries, such as France, have been pressing for a return to a multi-polar world as a means of hemming in the United States. But multi-polarity has its problems, one of which is that it has historically proven unstable and led to war.

An alternate way of organizing the international system is through a unipolar power like the United States. Many regions of the world and periods in history have seen stability under hegemony because a hegemon can exert a stabilizing or ordering influence on the international system by performing some of the functions of a central government. But there is a caveat. The unipolar power must use multilateral methods in order to increase the legitimacy of its international actions, lessen the possibility of imperial over-stretch, and prevent the destabilizing impact of other powers reacting against the hegemon's power and rising up to meet it. Multilateralist methods are especially necessary today because of the nature of the threat with which the Western world is dealing. "As the al Qaeda movement dissolves into virtuality in 60 countries worldwide, international cooperation becomes ever more indispensable to countering the threat."[38] The critical importance of intelligence, especially, is one of the main reasons the United States needs allies. Working through multilateral institutions is also important because it diffuses responsibility for international intervention and thus reduces the risk of an anti-American backlash.

The wider civilian requirements of the war on terrorism, in turn, point to Canada's diplomatic role in guaranteeing the security of its citizens. How does Canada fit into the American empire? The question is often posed, and the answer is relatively simple. The numerous inextricable links between Canada and the United

States dictate that the security of the Canadian homeland is tied to that of America. The practical requirements are innumerable homeland security and defence initiatives, as well as certain military capabilities abroad. But these are also strategic requirements. America's approach to the world directly impacts the security of Canadians; therefore, Canada needs to diplomatically engage America in order to urge it along a multilateral path and to encourage it to exercise its unipolar power through multilateral, rather than unilateral, means. If Canada is to be heard by the United States it needs to acquire sufficient credibility, and in Washington the currency of credibility is vigilant homeland security measures as well as robust military capabilities for the CF at home and abroad. Directly and indirectly, tactically and strategically, these are the elements on which Canadian security depends.

Glossary

ABM	Anti-ballistic Missile
AGS	Air-Ground Surveillance
AWACS	Airborne Early Warning and Control System
BMD	Ballistic Missile Defence
BMEWS	Ballistic Missile Early Warning System
BUR	*Bottom-Up Review*
CF	Canadian Forces
C4I	Command, Control, Communications, Computing, and Intelligence
CIA	Central Intelligence Agency
CONAD	US Continental Air Defense Command
CSBA	Canada Border Services Agency
CSE	Communications Security Establishment
CSIS	Canadian Security Intelligence Service
DCI	Director of Central Intelligence
DND	Department of National Defence
DSP	Defence Support Program
EHF	Extremely High Frequency
EPC	Emergency Preparedness Canada
FAST	Free and Secure Trade
FBI	Federal Bureau of Investigation
FEMA	Federal Emergency Management Agency
FINTRAC	Financial Transactions and Reports Analysis Centre
GPALS	Global Protection against Limited Strikes
GPS	Global Positioning System
IBETS	Integrated Border Enforcement Teams
INSETS	Integrated National Security Enforcement Teams

ISR	Intelligence, Surveillance, and Reconnaissance
ISTAR	Intelligence, Surveillance, Target Acquisition, and Reconnaissance
JSTARS	Joint Surveillance Target Attack Radar System
JTF	Joint Task Force
LAV	Light Armoured Vehicle
MCDV	Maritime Coastal Defence Vessels
MIDAS	Missile Defense Alarm System
NBC	Nuclear, Biological, Chemical
NMD	National Missile Defence
NORAD	North American Aerospace Defense Command
NORTHCOM	Northern Command
NWS	North Warning System
OCIPEP	Office of Critical Infrastructure Protection and Emergency Preparedness
PAVE PAWS	Phased-Array Warning System
PSEPC	Public Safety and Emergency Preparedness Canada
QDR	*Quadrennial Defense Review*
SBIRS	Space-Based Infrared System
SBR	Space-Based Radar
SDI	*Strategic Defense Initiative*
SDR	Strategic Defence Review
SIGINT	Signals Intelligence
SOF	Special Operations Force
SPACECOM	US Space Command
SPADATS	Space Detection and Tracking System
SPASUR	US Naval Space Command Space Surveillance System
SSPARS	Solid State Phased-Array Radar Systems
STSS	Space Tracking and Surveillance System
UAV	Unmanned Aerial Vehicle
US-VISIT	United States Visitor and Immigrant Status Indicator Technology
VACIS	Vehicle and Cargo Inspection System
WMD	Weapons of Mass Destruction

Notes

INTRODUCTION

1 Quoted in Buzan, *People, States and Fear: An Agenda for International Security Studies in the Post–Cold War Era*, 17.
2 This definition is adapted from Ullman, "Redefining Security," 133.
3 Dewitt and Leyton-Brown, *Canada's International Security Policy*, 4.
4 R.B. Byers, quoted in Dewitt and Leyton-Brown, *Canada's International Security Policy*, 2.
5 See Dewitt and Leyton-Brown, *Canada's International Security Policy*. The Martin government's international policy statement, *A Role of Pride and Influence in the World*, is the closest Canada has come to a national security strategy. Although more heavily informed by a security perspective than previous foreign policy statements, it is still somewhat broader in scope than a national security strategy. *Securing an Open Society: Canada's National Security Policy* is narrower in scope and can be compared to America's *National Strategy for Homeland Security* (Robert Wright, former national security adviser, comments to students in a class on defence policy in North America at Carleton University, Ottawa, 5 April 2005).

CHAPTER ONE

1 For an overview of early references to elements of offence-defence theory, see Lynn-Jones, "Offense-Defense Theory and Its Critics," 660; and Van Evera, *Causes of War: Power and the Roots of Conflict*, 118.
2 Jervis, "Cooperation under the Security Dilemma," 187.

3 See Wright, *A Study of War.*

4 Jervis, "Cooperation" (originally published in the journal *World Politics* in January 1978); see also Quester, *Offense and Defense in the International System.*

5 See Lynn-Jones, "Offense-Defense Theory," 661; and Glaser and Kaufmann, "What Is the Offense-Defense Balance and Can We Measure It?" 44–5.

6 Lynn-Jones, "Offense-Defense Theory," 661.

7 Ibid., 663.

8 Glaser and Kaufmann, "What Is the Offense-Defense Balance?" 45.

9 Lynn-Jones, "Offense-Defense Theory," 663.

10 Van Evera, "Offense, Defense and the Causes of War," 5.

11 Glaser and Kaufmann, "What Is the Offense-Defense Balance?" 47.

12 Dougherty and Pfaltzgraff, *Contending Theories of International Relations,* 90.

13 Jervis, "Cooperation," 71.

14 Glaser and Kaufmann, "What Is the Offense-Defense Balance?" 46.

15 Lynn-Jones, "Offense-Defense Theory," 674.

16 Gilpin, *War and Change in World Politics,* 62.

17 Glaser and Kaufmann, "What Is the Offense-Defense Balance?" 53.

18 Ibid., 59.

19 Jervis, "Cooperation," 77–8.

20 Glaser and Kaufmann, "What Is the Offense-Defense Balance?" 19.

21 Levy, "The Offensive/Defensive Balance of Military Technology: A Theoretical and Historical Analysis," 223.

22 Glaser and Kaufmann, "What Is the Offense-Defense Balance?" 46; and Van Evera, *Causes of War,* 160–5.

23 Glaser and Kaufmann, "What Is the Offense-Defense Balance?" 64.

24 Van Evera, *Causes of War,* 163.

25 See Lynn-Jones, "Offense-Defense Theory," for a detailed examination and rebuttal of the arguments in this area.

26 Levy, "Offensive/Defensive Balance," 225.

27 Glaser and Kaufmann, "What Is the Offense-Defense Balance?" 62.

28 Ibid., 69.

29 Lynn-Jones, "Offense-Defense Theory," 665.

CHAPTER TWO

1 Tenet, "Worldwide Threat – Converging Dangers in a Post 9/11 World." The DCI was previously the head of the entire intelligence

community and also the director of the CIA. The new post of
director of national intelligence has replaced the position of DCI.

2 Dougherty and Pfaltzgraff, *Contending Theories of International
Relations*, 387.

3 Cronin, "Rethinking Sovereignty: American Grand Strategy
in the Age of Terrorism," 121.

4 Tenet, "The Worldwide Threat in 2003: Evolving Dangers
in a Complex World."

5 US Department of State, *Patterns of Global Terrorism 2002*.

6 Bowers, "Al Qaeda's Profile: Slimmer but Menacing."

7 Quoted in Lumpkin, "US Says New Qaeda Figure Emerges."

8 Tenet, "Worldwide Threat in 2003."

9 Tenet, "The Worldwide Threat in 2004: Challenges in a Changing
Global Context." See also Goss, testimony before the Senate Armed
Services Committee.

10 See "MI5 Chief: Defeating Islamic Terror Will Be a Long Haul";
and Stern, "The Protean Enemy."

11 Oxford Research Group, quoted in McGrory, "Two Years On,
Bush May Be Losing War to Al Qaeda."

12 Lumpkin, "US Says New Qaeda Figure Emerges"; and Johnston
and Sanger, "New Generation of Leaders Is Emerging for Al Qaeda."

13 See Lumpkin, "US Says New Qaeda Figure Emerges"; Lumpkin,
"US Says Al Qaeda Hurt But Not Broken"; Farah and Priest, "Bin
Laden Son Plays Key Role in Al Qaeda"; and Gutkin, "Al-Qaida
Replacing Leaders."

14 Bearden, "Bin Laden's Capture Would Not Stop Al Qaeda."

15 Tenet, "Worldwide Threat in 2004."

16 See Tenet, "Worldwide Threat – Converging Dangers"; and
McGrory, "Two Years On."

17 World Markets Research Centre, London, *Global Terrorism Index
2003/04*, as reported in Prothero, "United States Ranked Fourth
as Likely Terrorist Target."

18 Tenet, "Worldwide Threat in 2004."

19 Falkenrath, "Confronting Nuclear, Biological and Chemical
Terrorism," 44–5.

20 Perry, "Preparing for the Next Attack," 32.

21 "The New Terrorism," 17.

22 Falkenrath, "Confronting Nuclear, Biological and Chemical
Terrorism," 56.

23 Cronin, "Rethinking Sovereignty," 123.

24 Gellman, "Qaeda Cyberterror Called Real Peril."

25 National Security Council, *National Security of the United States.*

26 US Department of State, *Patterns of Global Terrorism 2003.*

27 Cronin, "Rethinking Sovereignty," 120.

28 Stern, "Protean Enemy."

29 Tenet, "Worldwide Threat in 2003."

30 Canadian Security Intelligence Service, *2001 Public Report.*

31 Calder, testimony before the Standing Senate Committee on National Security and Defence.

32 Chalk and Rosenau, *Confronting the "Enemy Within": Security Intelligence, the Police, and Counterterrorism in Four Democracies,* 26.

33 Elcock, speech to the Vancouver Board of Trade.

34 Ibid.

35 Standing Senate Committee on National Security and Defence, *Defence of North America: A Canadian Responsibility.*

36 Chase, "US Terrorist Advisory Targets Canadian Flights."

37 Stephen Flynn, comments made at the conference "The Canada-US Partnership: Enhancing Our Common Security," Washington, DC, 14 March 2005.

38 The other countries named were Britain, France, Italy, Germany, and Australia.

39 Canadian Security Intelligence Service, *2002 Public Report.*

40 Bell, "Dangers for Canada Are Real."

41 Robert Wright, former national security adviser, comments to students in a class on defence policy in North America at Carleton University, Ottawa, 5 April 2005.

42 Canadian Security Intelligence Service, *2002 Public Report.*

43 Ibid.

44 Information warfare is also included as a type of asymmetric threat.

45 Tenet, "Worldwide Threat in 2003."

46 Tenet, "Worldwide Threat – Converging Dangers"; and Tenet, "Worldwide Threat in 2003."

47 US Commission on Weak States and National Security, *On the Brink: Weak States and National Security.*

48 Tenet, "Worldwide Threat in 2003."

49 Lewis, "The Roots of Muslim Rage," 49.

50 Doran, "Somebody Else's Civil War," 30.

51 "The Next War, They Say."

52 Hashim, "The World According to Usama Bin Laden."

53 Lewis, "License to Kill," 14.

54 Posen, "The Struggle against Terrorism: Grand Strategy, Strategy, and Tactics."
55 Walt, "Beyond Bin Laden," 70.
56 Stern, "Protean Enemy."
57 Lewis, "Roots of Muslim Rage," 52.
58 Purdy, "Countering Terrorism: The Missing Pillar," 23.
59 Lewis, "Roots of Muslim Rage," 48.
60 Stairs, "9/11 Terrorism, Root Causes and All That: Policy Implications of the Socio-cultural Argument," 8.
61 Hashim, "World According to Usama Bin Laden."
62 Simon, "The New Terrorism: Securing the Nation against a Messianic Foe."
63 Rubin, "The Real Roots of Arab Anti-Americanism," 73.
64 Ibid.
65 "Survey of Islam and the West," 5.
66 Huntington, "The Clash of Civilizations?"
67 "Next War."
68 Rubin, "Real Roots," 74.
69 "Survey of Islam," 6.
70 Krueger, "Poverty Doesn't Create Terrorists."
71 Simon, "New Terrorism."
72 Bertrand, "Fighting Islamic Terrorism: An Indirect Strategic Approach," 18. The term "good governance" is used here to refer to stable and representative governments that implement the rule of law, manage resources transparently, and deliver services effectively.
73 "Survey of Islam," 11.
74 Ibid., 6.
75 "Worldwide Web of Nuclear Danger," 26.
76 Lederer, "US Sees Nuclear Network Threat."
77 Reid, "Forty States 'Have Nuclear Capability.'"
78 Garrett, "The Nightmare of Bioterrorism," 76.
79 Ellis, "The Best Defense: Counterproliferation and US National Security," 120.
80 Tenet, "Worldwide Threat in 2003."
81 Falkenrath, "Confronting Nuclear, Biological and Chemical Terrorism," 54.
82 Tenet, "Worldwide Threat – Converging Dangers."
83 Canadian Security Intelligence Service, 2002 Public Report.
84 Tenet, "Worldwide Threat – Converging Dangers."

85 Mintz, "US Officials Warn of New Tactics by Al Qaeda."

86 Bronskill, "Spy Agency Sure Bin Laden Intent on Going Nuclear."

87 Innes, "Terrorists 'Would Use WMD if They Could.'"

88 Quoted in "Warning about WMD."

89 Betts, "The New Threat of Mass Destruction," 32.

90 Barrett, "US Study: Growing Threat from Ballistic Missiles," 34.

91 Perry, "Preparing for the Next Attack," 33.

92 Gedda, "North Korean Nuclear Missiles Could Reach US, Officials Fear."

93 Barrett, "US Study," 34.

94 Graham, "North Korea Is Used to Justify System."

95 Sokolski, "Rethinking Bio-chemical Dangers," 211–13.

96 John Parachini, "Putting WMD Terrorism into Perspective."

97 Betts, "New Threat," 32.

98 Simon, "New Terrorism."

CHAPTER THREE

1 The other dangers listed are regional dangers involving the threat of large-scale aggression by major regional powers; dangers to democracy and reform in the former Soviet Union and Eastern Europe; and economic dangers to national security that could result if America failed to build a strong, competitive economy.

2 Department of Defense, *Joint Vision 2010*, 10–11.

3 Department of Defense, *Quadrennial Defense Review* (1997), accessed 15 April 2005, <www.defenselink.mil/pubs/qdr/>.

4 Ibid.

5 Ibid.

6 National Defense Panel, *Transforming Defense: National Security in the 21st Century*, i, ii.

7 Ibid., ii.

8 National Security Council, *National Security Strategy for a New Century*, iii.

9 Ibid., iv.

10 U.S. Commission on National Security/21st Century, *New World Coming*, 4 (emphasis added).

11 U.S. Commission on National Security/21st Century, *Seeking a National Strategy*, 5.

12 U.S. Commission on National Security/21st Century, *Road Map for National Security: Imperative for Change*, viii (emphasis in original).

13 Department of Defense, *Quadrennial Defense Review* (2001), 11.

14 Ibid., 17.

15 Ibid., 18.

16 National Security Council, *National Security of the United States*, cover letter.

17 Against this argument the case has been made that there is no evidence that rogue states cannot be deterred from employing WMD through credible threats of unacceptable retaliation. See Record, *Bounding the Global War on Terrorism*, 42.

18 National Security Council, *National Security of the United States*, cover letter.

19 High-Level Panel on Threats, Challenges and Change, *A More Secure World: Our Shared Responsibility*, 54.

20 International law on the pre-emptive use of military force is often traced to the *Caroline* case of 1837, in which it was established that permissible pre-emptive self-defence requires the state to demonstrate that the "necessity of self-defence is instant [and] overwhelming, leaving no choice of means, and no moment of deliberation" (Secretary of State Daniel Webster, quoted in Arend, "International Law and the Preemptive Use of Military Force," 91).

21 High-Level Panel on Threats, Challenges and Change, *More Secure World*, 57–8.

22 Evans, "When Is It Right to Fight?" 76–7.

23 Posen, "The Struggle against Terrorism: Grand Strategy, Strategy, and Tactics," 45.

CHAPTER FOUR

1 These are my own definitions. Canada has yet to develop definitions of "homeland security" and "homeland defence." The United States defines "homeland security" as the prevention, pre-emption, and deterrence of, and defence against, aggression targeted at US territory, sovereignty, domestic population, and infrastructure as well as the management of the consequences of such aggression and other domestic emergencies. It defines "homeland defence" as the protection of US territory, domestic population, and critical infrastructure against military attacks emanating from outside the country.

2 The Office of Homeland Security, renamed the Homeland Security Council, remains in place to advise the president.

3 See Krim, "Cyber-security to Get Higher Profile Leader."

4 Segal, "After So Much Spent on Security, Are We Secure Yet?"

5 Betts, "Fixing Intelligence," 54.

6 International Institute for Strategic Studies, "US Intelligence Reform."

7 The US intelligence community comprises five agencies in their entirety, as well as the intelligence components of ten other departments or agencies. The former include the CIA, Defense Intelligence Agency (part of the DoD), National Geospatial-Intelligence Agency (part of the DoD), National Reconnaissance Office (part of the DoD), and National Security Agency (part of the DoD). The latter include army intelligence, navy intelligence, air force intelligence, Marine Corps intelligence, Coast Guard intelligence, the Department of Energy, Department of Homeland Security, Department of State, Department of the Treasury, and FBI (part of the Department of Justice). The post of DCI (head of the entire intelligence community and director of the CIA), has now become that of director of national intelligence.

8 Matthews, "Momentum Builds for Single US Intel Chief," 6.

9 Shenon, "US to Put Inspectors at Muslim Ports."

10 Fife, "Terrorism Draws Us Closer to US"

11 Matthews, "US Watches for Cargo Use by Terrorists."

12 Kime, "US Coast Guard Could Lose Security Duties," 32; and Collins, "Change and Continuity: The US Coast Guard Today," 11.

13 Flynn, "The Neglected Home Front," 22.

14 Dinsmore, "Don't Let Ports Be Weakest Link."

15 Quoted in Record, Bounding the Global War on Terrorism, 43.

16 Nickerson, "US-Canada Security Brings Frustration to Both Sides of Border."

17 "US Launches Aerial Surveillance of Border."

18 Matthews, "US Lawmakers Push 'Prompt Global Strike': Homeland UAVs, Special Forces Also Winners in 2004 Authorization Bill," 4.

19 Kaufman and Blair, "UAV Makers See Growing Homeland Security Market," 8.

20 Berger, "Unmanned Aerial Vehicles on Patrol at US-Mexico Border," 28.

21 "Update on Preparedness."

22 Cox, "Intercepting Bioterrorism."

23 Mintz, "Bioterrorism Procedures Are Outlined: Bush Directive Specifies Agency Responsibilities."

24 Taylor and Ramstack, "Ridge Adds 5,000 Air Marshals to Help Get 'Surge Capacity.'"
25 Mintz, "Homeland Security Boosts Funds on Antimissile Plan."
26 Lichtblau, "Government Report on US Aviation Warns of Security Holes."
27 Axtman, "New Tracking System to Safeguard Borders"; and Lambro, "Pre-emptive Security."
28 "Cutting through the Red Tape: US Intelligence Reform," 26.
29 Eggen, "FBI Applies New Rules to Surveillance."
30 Seper, "FBI 'Reprioritized' after '01 Terror Attacks, Report Says."
31 Risen, "Ex-government Officials Recommend Intelligence Overhaul."
32 Chalk and Rosenau, Confronting the "Enemy Within": Security Intelligence, the Police, and Counterterrorism in Four Democracies, 43–4, 48.
33 National Commission on Terrorist Attacks upon the United States, The 9/11 Commission Report, 423–4.
34 From the OCIPEP Web site, accessed December 2004, <www.ocipep.gc.ca>.
35 Rudner, "Contemporary Threats, Future Tasks: Canadian Intelligence and the Challenges of Global Security," 141–2.
36 Hurst, "Canada Listens to World as Partner in Spy System."
37 Elcock, speech to the Canadian Association for Security and Intelligence Studies Conference.
38 Ward Elcock, quoted in Bell, "CSIS Admits to Spying Abroad."
39 At least one Canadian former member of the Permanent Joint Board on Defence has acknowledged feeling like "the Canadian freeloader" because he did not have intelligence of equal value to offer in exchange for the intelligence he was seeking. See Standing Senate Committee on National Security and Defence, Canadian Security and Military Preparedness, 61.
40 Standing Committee on National Defence and Veterans Affairs, Facing Our Responsibilities: The State of Readiness of the Canadian Forces, chapter 2.
41 Humphreys, "Border Guards See Policing as Main Role."
42 Margaret Bloodworth, deputy minister of PSEPC, comments to students in a class on defence policy in North America at Carleton University, Ottawa, 8 March 2005.
43 Jon Allen, Embassy of Canada in the United States, comments made at the conference "The Canada-US Partnership: Enhancing Our Common Security," Washington, DC, 14 March 2005.

44 Maher, "Boost for Coast Guard Expected."
45 For a more detailed discussion of the *Anti-terrorism Act* and the
    Public Safety Act, see Roach, *September 11: Consequences for Canada.*
46 *"Public Safety Act* Receives Royal Assent," Government of Canada
    news release, 6 May 2004.
47 Martin Rudner, paraphrased in Bell, "Dangers for Canada
    Are Real."
48 Bell, "Terrorist Fundraising Tripled in Canada This Year: Report."
49 Seper, "Guarding America's Border."
50 Kennedy, testimony before the Standing Senate Committee
    on National Security and Defence.
51 Auditor General of Canada, *National Security: The 2001
    Anti-terrorism Initiative,* para. 3.149.
52 Standing Senate Committee on National Security and Defence,
    The Longest Under-Defended Borders in the World.
53 Michael O'Hanlon of the Brookings Institution, quoted in
    Matthews, "US Watches for Cargo Use," 8.
54 See Standing Senate Committee on National Security and Defence,
    Canadian Security.
55 Standing Senate Committee on National Security and Defence,
    Longest Under-Defended Borders.
56 Agencies involved include the Pentagon, the Canadian Navy,
    the Departments of State and Justice in the US, the Canadian
    Department of Foreign Affairs, and the RCMP, among others.
57 Government of Canada, *Securing an Open Society,* 39.
58 "Security and Prosperity Partnership of North America Established."
59 "More Troops to Afghanistan."
60 Government of Canada, *Canada's International Policy Statement,
    A Role of Pride and Influence in the World,* 9.
61 Ward Elcock, comments to students in a class on defence policy in
    North America at Carleton University, Ottawa, 24 February 2004.
62 Tibbetts, "Our Border 'Not a Conduit for Terrorists.'"
63 Senator Tommy Banks, in a question to CSIS Director Ward Elcock
    during testimony before the Standing Senate Committee on
    National Security and Defence, 17 February 2003.
64 Rekai, *United States and Canadian Immigration Policies: Marching
    Together to Different Tunes.*
65 Tibbetts, "Our Border."
66 Bilodeau, testimony before the Standing Senate Committee
    on National Security and Defence.

67 "'Safe Third Country' Agreement to be Signed This Week."

68 Wright, testimony before the Standing Senate Committee on National Security and Defence.

69 The only exception is that in a family reunification case, the claimant could be exempted from the requirement of making a claim in the first country of arrival.

70 Manley, Aspe, and Weld, *Creating a North American Community*, 10.

71 Robert Wright, former national security adviser, comments to students in a class on defence policy in North America at Carleton University, Ottawa, 5 April 2005.

72 For example, a national cyberspace strategy. Keith Coulter, former CSE chief, comments to students in a class on defence policy in North America at Carleton University, Ottawa, 10 March 2003.

73 Cooperation between Canada and the United States for the defence of North America is often dated to a meeting between Prime Minister Mackenzie King and President Franklin Roosevelt held in Kingston, Ontario, in August 1938. The two leaders were there to mark the opening of an international bridge between Canada and the US. In his speech Roosevelt stated that the United States would not stand idly by if Canadian soil were threatened (he was thinking of Japan). King responded that Canada would ensure that no enemy forces made their way by land, sea, or air to the United States across Canadian territory.

74 Ljunggren, "Ottawa Vows to Do More to Prevent Attacks on US."

CHAPTER FIVE

1 The functional commands are Joint Forces Command, Special Operations Command, Transportation Command, and Strategic Command. The geographic commands are Northern Command, Southern Command, European Command, Pacific Command, and Central Command.

2 "Pentagon Realigns Military Structure."

3 Literally, "the power or authority of the county." See Felicetti and Luce, "The *Posse Comitatus Act*: Liberation from the Lawyers," 95.

4 Carafano, *Citizen-Soldiers and Homeland Security: A Strategic Assessment*, 8.

5 Boyer, "Troops for Border Sought."

6 Office of Homeland Security, *National Strategy for Homeland Security*, 48.

7 <www.northcom.mil>.

8 Felicetti and Luce, *"Posse Comitatus Act,"* 94.

9 US Commission on National Security/21st Century, *Road Map for National Security: Imperative for Change,* ix.

10 Carafano, *Citizen-Soldiers,* 8. The National Guard can be called into federal service under title 10 or 32 of the US Code.

11 "NORAD Could Evolve into North American NATO, Says US Military Leader."

12 Sherman, "US Drafts Homeland Strategy," 1.

13 Ibid.

14 Government of Canada, *Canada's International Policy Statement: A Role of Pride and Influence in the World,* 18.

15 Ibid.

16 Department of National Defence, *Report on Plans and Priorities 2003–04.*

17 This section states that the CF can "be called out for service in aid of the civil power in any case in which a riot or disturbance of the peace, beyond the powers of the civil authorities to suppress, prevent or deal with and requiring that service, occurs or is, in the opinion of an attorney general, considered as likely to occur."

18 Most radar, using technology developed during World War II, is limited to about ninety kilometres because the waves travel in a straight line and cannot "see" over the horizon; but the surface wave radar uses advanced technology to travel along the curvature of the Earth.

19 Wattie, "Radar Stations to Guard Canada by Sea." There is some concern that the system could interfere with civilian radio transmissions and that therefore the frequency will have to change, possibly impacting on how the network performs. See Pugliese, "Anti-terror Radar Plan Tied Up in Red Tape."

20 "Deep-Sea Tripwire to Nab Terrorists."

21 Forcier, interview, 30.

22 Pugliese, "Canada to Try UAVs in Arctic," 14.

23 In 2004 the government announced that the CF will buy twenty-eight Sikorsky H92 maritime helicopters; however, the first will not arrive until 2008.

24 Naval officers aboard the HMCS *Athabaskan,* on exercise off Jacksonville, Florida, conversations with the author, 18–21 February 2005.

25 Pugliese, "Navy Shops around for New Midsized Patrol Vessels."

26 Meisner, testimony before the Standing Senate Committee on National Security and Defence.

27 Williams, testimony before the Standing Senate Committee on National Security and Defence.

28 Cleverley, "Navies Will Join Coast Guards in Exercise."

29 Pugliese, "Overhaul Will Boost Canada's Coastal Security," 36.

30 Paraskevas, "Make Coast Guard an Armed Military Force, Committee Urges."

31 Standing Senate Committee on National Security and Defence, *The Longest Under-Defended Borders in the World.*

32 Buck, testimony before the Standing Senate Committee on National Security and Defence.

33 See Griffiths, "The Shipping News: Canada's Arctic Sovereignty Not on Thinning Ice."

34 See Huebert, "The Shipping News Part II: How Canada's Arctic Sovereignty Is on Thinning Ice."

35 Office of Naval Research, *Naval Operations in an Ice-Free Arctic.*

36 Government of Canada, *Canada's International Policy Statement*, 7.

37 For example, Denmark. See Carlson, "North Pole a Hot Spot."

38 VanderKlippe, "Arctic a Potential Terror Target."

39 Humphreys, "Canada's Troops to Reclaim Arctic."

40 Standing Committee on National Defence and Veterans Affairs, *Facing Our Responsibilities: The State of Readiness of the Canadian Forces*, 66.

41 Gimblett, testimony before the Standing Senate Committee on National Security and Defence.

42 Wattie, "Forces to 'Flex Muscles' in North."

43 Auld, "Coast Guard Icebreaker Aging Gracelessly."

44 Government of Canada, *Canada's International Policy Statement*, 13.

45 Minister's Monitoring Committee, *In the Service of the Nation: Canada's Citizen Soldiers for the 21st Century.*

46 Standing Senate Committee on National Security and Defence, *Canadian Security and Military Preparedness*, 27, 30.

47 Morton, "'No More Disagreeable or Onerous Duty': Canadians and Military Aid of the Civil Power, Past, Present, Future."

48 Department of National Defence, *1994 Defence White Paper*, 45.

49 Quoted in Vice Chief of the Defence Staff, *Rethinking the Total Force: Aligning the Defence Team for the 21st Century.*

50 David Price, former parliamentary secretary to Pratt, paraphrased in Wattie, "Reservists Touted as Terrorism Fighters."

51 Major General Edward Fitch, paraphrased in Slobodian, "General Sees Reserve Force as Vital for Terror Response."

52 Standing Senate Committee on National Security and Defence, *Canadian Security*, 97.

53 Pugliese, "Part-Time Soldiers to Play Key Role in Civil Defence."

54 Fraser, *Progress Report on Land Force Reserve Restructure.*

55 Fitch, "Army Reserves in Homeland Defence."

56 Paraphrased in Vice Chief of the Defence Staff, *Rethinking the Total Force.*

57 British Ministry of Defence, *The Strategic Defence Review: A New Chapter*, 25–6.

58 See Falkenrath, "Confronting Nuclear, Biological and Chemical Terrorism."

59 Government of Canada, *Canada's International Policy Statement*, 12–13.

60 Ibid., 19–20.

61 By contrast, on 11 September 2001, FAA flight controllers took fifteen minutes to notify NORAD that they thought a flight out of Boston had been hijacked, leaving NORAD only six minutes to respond before the plane hit the World Trade Center.

62 Kelly, "Defense Hub Is Scouring Sky for Next Sneak Attack."

63 Canadian Forces Publication B-GL-300–003/FP-000 (Command), 59.

64 Lindsey, "Potential Contributions by the Canadian Armed Forces to the Defence of North America against Terrorism," 326.

65 National Commission on Terrorist Attacks upon the United States, *The 9/11 Commission Report*, 16, 22.

66 Lindsey, "Canada, North American Security, and NORAD," 3.

67 Government of Canada, *Canada's International Policy Statement*, 19.

68 Graham, "US Urged to Broaden Defense against Terrorist Missiles."

69 Mason, *Canadian Defense Priorities: What Might the United States Like to See?* 4.

70 Tirpak, "The Space Based Radar Plan."

71 Goodman, "Space-Based Radar Heads to Next Stage."

72 In the 1950s the US Air Force developed the Bomarc missile as a long-range interceptor missile against aircraft, but it was phased out by 1964 (Bruce-Briggs, *The Shield of Faith*, 266). Because these missiles had nuclear warheads, and because some of the sites were located in Canada, the Bomarc was the subject of significant political controversy in Canada.

73 Auditor General of Canada, "National Defence – Upgrading the CF-18 Fighter Aircraft," 7.

74 Lieutenant General Ken Pennie, chief of the air staff, comments made at the Centre for Security and Defence Studies, Carleton University, Ottawa, 29 November 2004.

75 Koring, "Canadian Air Defence Lags behind US after Sept. 11."

76 Lindsey, "Canada, North American Security, and NORAD," 2.

77 Lindsey, "Potential Contributions," 316.

78 Defense Science Board, *2003 Summer Study on DoD Roles and Missions in Homeland Security*, xii.

79 Sherman, "US Drafts Homeland Strategy," 8.

80 Lieutenant-General Edward Anderson, deputy commander of Northern Command, remarks to a conference on Homeland Defence and Land Force Reserves, University of Calgary, 26 March 2004.

81 Alberts, "Canada, US Study Response to Attacks on Parliament Hill."

82 Naval officers aboard the HMCS *Athabaskan*, on exercise off Jacksonville, Florida, conversations with the author, 18–21 February 2005; and Colonel Mike Haché, DND director of western hemisphere policy, comments to students in a class on defence policy in North America at Carleton University, Ottawa, 15 March 2005.

83 Rear Admiral Ian Mack, comments made at the conference "The Canada-US Partnership: Enhancing Our Common Security," Washington, DC, 14 March 2005.

84 Huebert, "Shipping News Part II," 297.

CHAPTER SIX

1 Center for Defense Information, *National Missile Defence: What Does It All Mean?* 2.

2 Cox, "Canada and Ballistic Missile Defence," 242.

3 This means that the satellites stay fixed with respect to their location above the Earth.

4 Lindsey, "Potential Contributions by the Canadian Armed Forces to the Defence of North America against Terrorism," 313.

5 Sirak, "America's BMD Stumbles," 23.

6 <http://www.Stnorthropgrumman.com>, accessed 12 December 2004.

7 Hackett, "Missile Defense on Track."

8 Cavas, "US Ships Begin Detect-and-Track Duties," 14.

9 Cox, "Canada and Ballistic Missile Defence," 244.

10 The surveillance network includes three transmitters and six receivers located at sites on an east-west great-circle path across the southern United States. It produces a fence of electromagnetic energy that can detect objects out to an effective range of 15,000 nautical miles.

11 Pugliese, "Canada to Develop Sensor to Track Satellites, Debris," 20.

12 Pugliese, "Canadian Project for Space-Based Sensor Moves to New Stage," 16.

13 Department of National Defence, *At a Crossroads: Annual Report of the Chief of the Defence Staff*, 40.

14 Fergusson, "National Missile Defense, Homeland Defense, and Outer Space: Policy Dilemmas in the Canada-US Relationship," 244, 251 n11.

15 Pugliese, "Canada Aims to Prove Value of Micro-Sats," 19.

16 Cox, "Canada and Ballistic Missile Defence," 247.

17 Sokolsky, "The Bilateral Defence Relationship with the United States," 179.

18 Murray, "NORAD and US Nuclear Operations," 228.

19 Sokolsky, "The Bilateral Defence Relationship with the United States," 183–4.

20 Fergusson, "National Missile Defense," 235.

21 Gertz, "Bush Approves Missile Defense."

22 Growing costs and slow progress may lead the Missile Defense Agency to abandon the airborne laser. See Ratnam, "Airborne Laser May Be Grounded."

23 Pugliese, "US Wants Weapons in Space."

24 A short-range missile has a range of 600 kilometres; a medium-range missile, 1,300 kilometres; an intermediate-range missile, 3,500 kilometres; and an intercontinental missile, 5,500 kilometres.

25 Sherman, "US Navy's Role Soars," 10.

26 "Warding off Missiles: An American Dream," 25.

27 Graham, "Missile Defense Agency Faulted on Testing and Accountability."

28 Sherman, "US Navy's Role Soars," 1.

29 Lagassé, *The SORT Debate: Implications for Canada.* See also Pugliese, "US Missile Plan Risks Arms Race, Canada Told."

30 For the distinction between "operational control" and "operational command," see chapter 5.

31 Jockel, *Four US Military Commands: NORTHCOM, NORAD, SPACECOM, STRATCOM – The Canadian Opportunity,* 4–5.

32 <http://www.stratcom.mil>.

33 Department of Foreign Affairs, "Canada and Ballistic Missile Defence."

34 Lieutenant General Joseph Inge, deputy commander of US Northern Command, comments made at the conference "The Canada-US Partnership: Enhancing Our Common Security," Washington, DC, 14 March 2005.

35 Jockel, "A Strong Friend Is a Good Defence."

36 Lieutenant General (retired) George MacDonald, former deputy commander of NORAD, quoted in Thorne, "NORAD Role Could Be Altered."

37 "Canada's Missile Role."

38 James Fergusson, director of the Centre for Defence and Security Studies, University of Manitoba, quoted in Pugliese, "Space Program Could Feed Data to Missile Shield."

CHAPTER SEVEN

1 Standing Committee on National Defence and Veterans Affairs, *Facing Our Responsibilities: The State of Readiness of the Canadian Forces.*

2 See, for example, "Define Canada's Global Agenda"; and "Where Paul Martin Should Lead Canada."

3 Conservative Party of Canada, *Demand Better Security: The Conservative Plan for Defence*; and Governor General of Canada, *Speech from the Throne.*

4 Canadian Security Intelligence Service, *2001 Public Report*. See also Canadian Security Intelligence Service, *2002 Public Report.*

5 British Ministry of Defence, *The Strategic Defence Review: A New Chapter*, 9.

6 Government of Canada, *Canada's International Policy Statement: A Role of Pride and Influence in the World*, 8.

7 Ibid., 17.

8 Kilian, "US Expanding Military Sites in Mideast, Asia: Network Counters 'Arc of Instability.'" See also Tyson, "New US Strategy: 'Lily Pad' Bases."

9 Cavas, "New Missions Will Rely on Sea Basing," 4.

10 Pugliese, "Canada to Improve CF-18s' Targeting, Weapons," 14.

11 Murray and Scales, *The Iraq War*, 243.

12 Government of Canada, *Canada's International Policy Statement*, 30.

13 General Rick Hillier, briefing on the defence component of *Canada's International Policy Statement*, Ottawa, 19 April 2005.

14 Hooton, "Naval Firepower Comes of Age."

15 British Ministry of Defence, *Strategic Defence Review*, 16.

16 Chao, NATO AGS – *Finally Ready to Fly?* 5.

17 The rapid acquisition of UAVs has forced some scheduling changes, because UAVs were originally to be among the last sensors acquired under ISTAR: "We had a plan, and we were going to buy all the communications links first and integrate all the sensors we have now ... [but] reality interfered with the plan." Brigadier General Peter Holt, quoted in Pugliese, "Canada Revises Sensor Program," 34.

18 Horn, "When Cultures Collide: The Conventional Military/ SOF Chasm," 3.

19 Murray and Scales, *Iraq War*, 69–70.

20 Scarborough, "Special Ops Steal Show as Successes Mount in Iraq."

21 America's special operations community will stand at more than 52,000 troops within the next few years, and its budget is already close to $7 billion. See Hammond, "Special Operations Forces: Relevant, Ready and Precise," 18.

22 Government of Canada, *Canada's International Policy Statement*, 12.

23 This is a minimum figure. Others have placed it closer to a total of 2,000 troops. See Brister, "Canadian Special Operations Forces: A Blueprint for the Future," 36.

24 Government of Canada, *Canada's International Policy Statement*, 13.

25 Donald Rumsfeld, quoted in Government of Canada, *Canada's International Policy Statement*.

26 Murray and Scales, *Iraq War*, 244.

27 Pugliese, "Canada Shifts Plan to Increase Special Forces," 14.

28 Svitak, "US Army, Navy Mull Lessons Learned in Afghanistan War," 38.

29 British Ministry of Defence, *Strategic Defence Review*, 17.

30 "Transformed? A Survey of the Defence Industry," 3.

31 Murray and Scales, *Iraq War*, 245.

32 Roosevelt, "Strykers Turning In 'Extraordinary Performance.'"

33 Naylor, "Overhauling the US Army," 8.

34 Loeb, "Army Expansion Could Last 5 Years."

35 Burger, "Fighting in the Streets."

36 British Ministry of Defence, *Strategic Defence Review*, 18.

37 Loeb, "Chief Hopes to Quicken Army's Shift."

38 Pugliese, "Canadian Navy Wins Nod for Sealift-Supply Vessels," 17.

39 MacKenzie, testimony before the Standing Senate Committee on National Security and Defence.

40 Harnden, "'Fight Light, Fight Fast' Theory Advances."

41 Koring, "Strength, Speed, Surprise: How Franks Won the War."

42 Gouré, "A Campaign like No Other in History: Initial Impressions of Operation Iraqi Freedom."

43 Matthews, "Triumph of Jointness," 1.

44 Sallot, "Graham Defends Joining US Arms Interception Plan."

45 "Present at the Creation: America's World Role," 14.

46 Sherman, "Global Teams Angle for Slice of Warship," 20.

47 Vickers, "LCS Could Bolster Defense against Terror," 28.

48 Government of Canada, *Canada's International Policy Statement*, 14.

49 Naval officers aboard the HMCS *Athabaskan*, on exercise off Jacksonville, Florida, conversations with the author, 18–21 February 2005.

50 Gimblett, testimony before the Standing Senate Committee on National Security and Defence, comments made by Senator Tommy Banks.

51 Naval officers aboard the HMCS *Athabaskan*, on exercise off Jacksonville, Florida, conversations with the author, 18–21 February 2005.

52 Government of Canada, *Canada's International Policy Statement*, 12.

53 Binnendijk and Johnson, *Transforming for Stabilization and Reconstruction Operations*, 98.

54 Murray and Scales, *Iraq War*, 97.

55 Stern, "Military 'Transformation' Might Not Mean Smaller Forces."

56 Graham, "Pentagon Considers Creating Postwar Peacekeeping Forces."

57 Binnendijk and Johnson, *Transforming for Stabilization*, 8.

58 Sherman, "US War on Terror Looms for QDR," 4.

59 For a detailed discussion of technologies to support military stabilization and reconstruction, see Binnendijk and Johnson, *Transforming for Stabilization*, 95–103.

CHAPTER EIGHT

1 Government of Canada, *Securing an Open Society: Canada's National Security Policy*, 50.

2 Simon, "The New Terrorism: Securing the Nation against a Messianic Foe."

3 Falkenrath, "Confronting Nuclear, Biological and Chemical Terrorism," 56.

4 Heymann, "Dealing with Terrorism," 33, 36.

5 Betts, "Fixing Intelligence," 44.

6 Heymann, "Dealing with Terrorism," 37.

7 Bowers, "Terror Still a No-Show on US Soil."

8 Bell, "Border Seen as Terrorist Focus."

9 Johnston and Stout, "Bin Laden Is Said to be Organizing for a US Attack."

10 Perry, "Preparing for the Next Attack," 36.

11 Betts, "Fixing Intelligence," 44.

12 Tomlinson, "Military Stalks Terrorists in Africa."

13 McLaughlin, "Why Sudan Has Become a Bush Priority."

14 Cronin, "Rethinking Sovereignty: American Grand Strategy in the Age of Terrorism," 134.

15 Crocker, "Engaging Failed States," 41.

16 Flynn, "The Neglected Home Front," 21.

17 Flynn, "America the Vulnerable," 64.

18 Parachini, "Putting WMD Terrorism into Perspective," 40.

19 Ellis, "The Best Defense: Counterproliferation and US National Security," 119.

20 Canadian Security Intelligence Service, 2002 *Public Report*.

21 Heymann, "Dealing with Terrorism," 32.

22 Simon, "New Terrorism."

23 Bowers, "Terror Still a No-Show."

24 Perry, "Preparing for the Next Attack," 35.

25 See Payne, *Deterrence in the Second Nuclear Age*.

26 Cronin, "Rethinking Sovereignty," 127.

27 Flynn, "Neglected Home Front," 21.

28 Cronin, "Rethinking Sovereignty," 130.

29 Payne, "NPR Moves US Beyond 'Balance of Terror,'" 29.

30 Perry, "Preparing for the Next Attack," 39.

31 Posen, "The Struggle against Terrorism: Grand Strategy, Strategy, and Tactics," 46.

32 US Secretary of Defense James Schlesinger, quoted in Sokolsky, "The Bilateral Defence Relationship with the United States," 176.

33 Bush, speech delivered at Pier 21. See also Bush, remarks on the War on Terror.

34 See, for example Ward, "Henault Hopes Defence Review Will Reveal What Government Expects, Will Pay."

35 Buck, testimony before the Standing Senate Committee on National Security and Defence, 6 December 2004.
36 Martin, address at CFB Gagetown.
37 Government of Canada, *Canada's International Policy Statement: A Role of Pride and Influence in the World*, 2.
38 Simon, "New Terrorism."

Bibliography

Alberts, Sheldon. "Canada, US Study Response to Attacks on Parliament Hill." *Ottawa Citizen*, 15 November 2003.

Arend, Anthony Clark. "International Law and the Preemptive Use of Military Force." *Washington Quarterly* 26, no. 2 (2003).

Art, Robert J., and Kenneth N. Waltz. *The Use of Force*. 4th ed. New York: University Press of America, 1993.

Auditor General of Canada. "National Defence – Upgrading the CF-18 Fighter Aircraft," chapter 3, *Report of the Auditor General of Canada*. Ottawa: Government of Canada, November 2004.

– *National Security: The 2001 Anti-terrorism Initiative*. Ottawa: Government of Canada, March 2004.

Auld, Alison. "Coast Guard Icebreaker Aging Gracelessly." *Canadian Press*, 15 December 2003.

Axtman, Kris. "New Tracking System to Safeguard Borders." *Christian Science Monitor*, 6 January 2004.

Barrett, Randy. "US Study: Growing Threat from Ballistic Missiles." *Defense News*, 13 October 2003.

Bearden, Milt. "Bin Laden's Capture Would Not Stop Al Qaeda." *International Herald Tribune*, 27 March 2004.

Bell, Stewart. "Border Seen as Terrorist Focus." *National Post*, 12 July 2004.

– "CSIS Admits to Spying Abroad." *National Post*, 20 October 2003.

– "Dangers for Canada Are Real." *National Post*, 15 October 2004.

– "Terrorist Fundraising Tripled in Canada This Year: Report." *Ottawa Citizen*, 5 November 2004.

Berger, Brian. "Unmanned Aerial Vehicles on Patrol at US-Mexico Border." *Defense News*, 13 September 2004.

Bertrand, Serge. "Fighting Islamic Terrorism: An Indirect Strategic Approach." *Canadian Military Journal* 3, no. 4 (2002–03).

Betts, Richard K. "Fixing Intelligence." *Foreign Affairs* 81, no. 1 (2002).

– "The New Threat of Mass Destruction." *Foreign Affairs* 77, no. 1 (1998).

Bilodeau, Ronald. Testimony before the Standing Senate Committee on National Security and Defence, 24 February 2003.

Binnendijk, Hans, and Stuart Johnson, eds. *Transforming for Stabilization and Reconstruction Operations.* Washington, DC: National Defense University, 2003.

Blanchfield, Mike. "Defence Chief to Alter the Way Military Works." *Ottawa Citizen*, 7 April 2005.

Bowers, Faye. "Al Qaeda's Profile: Slimmer but Menacing." *Christian Science Monitor*, 9 September 2003.

– "Terror Still a No-Show on US Soil." *Christian Science Monitor*, 5 January 2004.

Boyer, Dave. "Troops for Border Sought." *Washington Times*, 19 June 2002.

Brister, Bernard J. "Canadian Special Operations Forces: A Blueprint for the Future." *Canadian Military Journal* 5, no. 3 (2004).

British Ministry of Defence. *The Strategic Defence Review: A New Chapter.* London: British Ministry of Defence, July 2002.

Bronskill, Jim. "Spy Agency Sure Bin Laden Intent on Going Nuclear." *Canadian Press*, 4 November 2004.

Bruce-Briggs, Bernard. *The Shield of Faith.* New York: Simon and Schuster, 1988.

Buck, Ron. Testimony before the Standing Senate Committee on National Security and Defence, 7 April 2003.

– Testimony before the Standing Senate Committee on National Security and Defence, 6 December 2004.

Burger, Kim. "Fighting in the Streets." *Jane's Defence Weekly*, 20 November 2002.

Bush, George W. Remarks on the War on Terror. Oak Ridge National Laboratory, Oak Ridge, Tennessee, 12 July 2004.

– Speech at Pier 21. Halifax, Nova Scotia, 1 December 2004.

Buzan, Barry. *People, States and Fear: An Agenda for International Security Studies in the Post–Cold War Era.* Boulder, CO: Lynne Rienner Publishers, 1991.

Calder, Kenneth. Testimony before the Standing Senate Committee on National Security and Defence, 25 October 2004.

"Canada's Missile Role." *Globe and Mail*, 9 January 2004.

Canadian Forces Publication B-GL-300–003/FP-000 (Command), 21 July 1996.

Canadian Security Intelligence Service. *2001 Public Report*. Ottawa: CSIS, 6 June 2002.

– *2002 Public Report*. Ottawa: CSIS, 5 June 2003.

Carafano, Jay. *Citizen-Soldiers and Homeland Security: A Strategic Assessment*. Arlington, VA: Lexington Institute, March 2004.

Carlson, Heather J. "North Pole a Hot Spot." *Washington Times*, 21 October 2004.

Cavas, Christopher P. "New Missions Will Rely on Sea Basing." *Defense News*, 17 January 2005.

– "US Ships Begin Detect-and-Track Duties." *Defense News*, 30 August 2004.

Center for Defense Information. *National Missile Defence: What Does It All Mean?* Washington, DC: Center for Defense Information, September 2000.

Chalk, Peter, and William Rosenau. *Confronting the "Enemy Within": Security Intelligence, the Police, and Counterterrorism in Four Democracies*. Santa Monica, CA: RAND Corporation, 2004.

Chao, Pierre A. *NATO AGS – Finally Ready to Fly?* Washington, DC: Center for Strategic and International Studies, June 2004.

Chase, Steven. "US Terrorist Advisory Targets Canadian Flights." *Globe and Mail*, 5 September 2003.

Cleverley, Bill. "Navies Will Join Coast Guards in Exercise." *Victoria Times Colonist*, 13 February 2005.

Collins, Thomas H. "Change and Continuity: The US Coast Guard Today." *US Naval War College Review* 57, no. 2 (2004).

Conservative Party of Canada. *Demand Better Security: The Conservative Plan for Defence*. Ottawa: Conservative Party of Canada, 31 May 2004.

Cox, Christopher. "Intercepting Bioterrorism." *Washington Times*, 12 July 2004.

Cox, David. "Canada and Ballistic Missile Defence." In *Fifty Years of Canada-United States Security Cooperation*, edited by Joel J. Sokolsky and Joseph T. Jockel. Lewiston, NY: Edwin Meller Press, 1992.

Crocker, Chester A. "Engaging Failed States." *Foreign Affairs* 82, no. 5 (2003).

Cronin, Audrey Kurth. "Rethinking Sovereignty: American Grand Strategy in the Age of Terrorism." *Survival* 44, no. 2 (2002).

"Cutting through the Red Tape: US Intelligence Reform." *Jane's Defence Weekly*, 23 October 2002.

"Deep-Sea Tripwire to Nab Terrorists." *Canadian Press*, 15 December 2003.

Defense Science Board. *2003 Summer Study on DoD Roles and Missions in Homeland Security*. Washington, DC: Defense Science Board, November 2003.

"Define Canada's Global Agenda." *Toronto Star*, 30 December 2003.

Department of Defense. *Bottom-Up Review*. Washington, DC: Department of Defense, 1993.

– *Joint Vision 2010*. Washington, DC: Department of Defense, 1996.

– *Quadrennial Defense Review*. Washington, DC: Department of Defense, 1997.

– *Quadrennial Defense Review*. Washington, DC: Department of Defense, 2001.

Department of Foreign Affairs. "Canada and Ballistic Missile Defence." *Backgrounder*, 15 February 2004.

Department of National Defence. *At a Crossroads: Annual Report of the Chief of the Defence Staff*. Ottawa: Department of National Defence, June 2002.

– *1994 Defence White Paper*. Ottawa: Department of National Defence, 1994.

– *Report on Plans and Priorities 2003–04*. Ottawa: Department of National Defence, 27 March 2003.

Dewitt, David B., and David Leyton-Brown, eds. *Canada's International Security Policy*. Scarborough, ON: Prentice Hall, 1995.

Dinsmore, M.R. "Don't Let Ports Be Weakest Link." *Christian Science Monitor*, 21 September 2004.

Doran, Michael Scott. "Somebody Else's Civil War." *Foreign Affairs* 81, no. 1 (2002).

Dougherty, James E., and Robert L. Pfaltzgraff Jr. *Contending Theories of International Relations*. 5th ed. New York: Addison Wesley Longman, 2001.

Eggen, Dan. "FBI Applies New Rules to Surveillance." *Washington Post*, 13 December 2003.

Elcock, Ward. Speech to the Canadian Association for Security and Intelligence Studies Conference, Vancouver, 16–18 October 2003.

– Speech to the Vancouver Board of Trade, 7 November 2002.

– Testimony before the Standing Senate Committee on National Security and Defence, 17 February 2003.

Ellis, Jason D. "The Best Defense: Counterproliferation and US National Strategy." *Washington Quarterly* 26, no. 2 (2003).

Evans, Gareth. "When Is It Right to Fight?" *Survival* 46, no. 3 (2004).

Falkenrath, Richard. "Confronting Nuclear, Biological and Chemical Terrorism." *Survival* 40, no. 3 (1998).

Farah, Douglas, and Dana Priest. "Bin Laden Son Plays Key Role in Al Qaeda." *Washington Post*, 14 October 2003.

Felicetti, Gary, and John Luce. "The *Posse Comitatus Act*: Liberation from the Lawyers." *Parameters* 34, no. 3 (2004).

Fergusson, James. "National Missile Defense, Homeland Defense, and Outer Space: Policy Dilemmas in the Canada-US Relationship." In *Canada among Nations 2001: The Axworthy Legacy*, edited by Fen Osler Hampson, Norman Hiller, and Maureen Appel Molot. Toronto: Oxford University Press, 2001.

Fife, Robert. "Terrorism Draws Us Closer to US." *Ottawa Citizen*, 15 October 2004.

Fitch, Edward. "Army Reserves in Homeland Defence." Speech to the Defence Associations Institute Conference, Ottawa, 27 February 2003.

Flynn, Stephen E. "America the Vulnerable." *Foreign Affairs* 81, no. 1 (2002).

– "The Neglected Home Front." *Foreign Affairs* 83, no. 5 (2004).

Forcier, Jean-Yves. Interview. *Defense News*, 3 May 2004.

Fraser, John. *Progress Report on Land Force Reserve Restructure*. Ottawa: Department of National Defence, February 2002.

Garrett, Laurie. "The Nightmare of Bioterrorism." *Foreign Affairs* 80, no. 1 (2001).

Gedda, George. "North Korean Nuclear Missiles Could Reach US, Officials Fear." *Toronto Star*, 12 September 2003.

Gellman, Barton. "Qaeda Cyberterror Called Real Peril." *International Herald Tribune*, 28 June 2002.

Gertz, Bill. "Bush Approves Missile Defense." *Washington Times*, 17 December 2002.

Gilpin, Robert. *War and Change in World Politics*. Cambridge: Cambridge University Press, 1981.

Gimblett, Richard. Testimony before the Standing Senate Committee on National Security and Defence, 21 February 2005.

Glaser, Charles L., and Chaim Kaufmann. "What Is the Offense-Defense Balance and Can We Measure It?" *International Security* 22, no. 4 (1988).

Goodman, Glenn W. "Space-Based Radar Heads to Next Stage." *Defense News*, 19 July 2004.

Goss, Porter J. Testimony before the Senate Armed Services Committee, 17 March 2005.

Gouré, Daniel. "A Campaign like No Other in History: Initial Impressions of Operation Iraqi Freedom." *San Diego Union-Tribune*, 20 April 2003.

Government of Canada. *Canada's International Policy Statement: A Role of Pride and Influence in the World*. Ottawa: Government of Canada, April 2005.

– *Securing an Open Society: Canada's National Security Policy.* Ottawa: Government of Canada, April 2004.

Governor General of Canada. *Speech from the Throne.* Ottawa: Government of Canada, 2 February 2004.

Graham, Bradley. "Missile Defense Agency Faulted on Testing and Accountability." *Washington Post,* 24 April 2004.

– "North Korea Is Used to Justify System." *Washington Post,* 29 September 2004.

– "Pentagon Considers Creating Postwar Peacekeeping Forces." *Washington Post,* 24 November 2003.

– "US Urged to Broaden Defense against Terrorist Missiles." *Washington Post,* 19 August 2002.

Griffiths, Franklin. "The Shipping News: Canada's Arctic Sovereignty Not on Thinning Ice." *International Journal* 58, no. 2 (2003).

Gutkin, Steven. "Al-Qaida Replacing Leaders." *Washington Post,* 16 October 2003.

Hackett, James T. "Missile Defense on Track." *Washington Times,* 9 September 2003.

Hammond, Jamie. "Special Operations Forces: Relevant, Ready and Precise." *Canadian Military Journal* 5, no. 3 (2004).

Harnden, Toby. "'Fight Light, Fight Fast' Theory Advances." *Daily Telegraph* (London), 14 April 2003.

Hashim, Ahmed. "The World According to Usama Bin Laden." *Naval War College Review* 54, no. 4 (2001).

Heymann, Philip B. "Dealing with Terrorism." *International Security* 26, no. 3 (2001–02).

High-Level Panel on Threats, Challenges and Change. *A More Secure World: Our Shared Responsibility.* New York: United Nations, 2004.

Hooton, Ted. "Naval Firepower Comes of Age." *Jane's Defence Weekly,* 13 November 2002.

Horn, Bernd. "When Cultures Collide: The Conventional Military/SOF Chasm." *Canadian Military Journal* 5, no. 3 (2004).

Huebert, Robert. "The Shipping News Part II: How Canada's Arctic Sovereignty Is on Thinning Ice." *International Journal* 58, no. 3 (2003).

Humphreys, Adrian. "Border Guards See Policing as Main Role." *National Post,* 1 February 2003.

– "Canada's Troops to Reclaim Arctic." *National Post,* 25 March 2004.

Huntington, Samuel. "The Clash of Civilizations?" *Foreign Affairs* 72, no. 3 (2003).

Hurst, Lynda. "Canada Listens to World as Partner in Spy System." *Toronto Star,* 7 March 2004.

Innes, John. "Terrorists 'Would Use WMD if They Could.'" *Scotsman*, 17 November 2003.

International Institute for Strategic Studies. "US Intelligence Reform." *IISS Strategic Comments* 10, no. 8 (2004).

Jehl, Douglas. "Administration Considers a Post for National Intelligence Director." *New York Times*, 15 April 2004.

Jervis, Robert. "Cooperation under the Security Dilemma." In *The Use of Force*, edited by Robert J. Art and Kenneth N. Waltz. 4th ed. New York: University Press of America, 1993.

Jockel, Joseph T. "A Strong Friend Is a Good Defence." *Globe and Mail*, 14 January 2004.

– *Four US Military Commands: NORTHCOM, NORAD, SPACECOM, STRATCOM – The Canadian Opportunity*. IRPP Working Paper 2003–03. Montreal: Institute for Research on Public Policy, 2003.

Johnston, David, and David E. Sanger. "New Generation of Leaders Is Emerging for Al Qaeda." *New York Times*, 10 August 2004.

– and David Stout. "Bin Laden Is Said to be Organizing for a US Attack." *New York Times*, 9 July 2004.

Kaufman, Gail, and Bridgette Blair. "UAV Makers See Growing Homeland Security Market." *Defense News*, 21 July 2003.

Kelly, David. "Defense Hub Is Scouring Sky for Next Sneak Attack." *Los Angeles Times*, 26 August 2004.

Kennedy, Paul. Testimony before the Standing Senate Committee on National Security and Defence, 24 February 2003.

Kilian, Michael. "US Expanding Military Sites in Mideast, Asia: Network Counters 'Arc of Instability.'" *Chicago Tribune*, 23 March 2004.

Kime, Patricia. "US Coast Guard Could Lose Security Duties." *Defense News*, 15 September 2003.

Koring, Paul. "Canadian Air Defence Lags behind US after Sept. 11." *Globe and Mail*, 18 June 2004.

– "Strength, Speed, Surprise: How Franks Won the War." *Globe and Mail*, 12 April 2003.

Krim, Jonathan. "Cyber-security to Get Higher Profile Leader." *Washington Post*, 13 October 2004.

Krueger, Alan B. "Poverty Doesn't Create Terrorists." *New York Times*, 29 May 2003.

Lagassé, Philippe. *The SORT Debate: Implications for Canada*. IRPP Working Paper 2003–01. Montreal: Institute for Research on Public Policy, 2003.

Lambro, Donald. "Pre-emptive Security." *Washington Times*, 8 January 2004.

Lederer, Edith M. "US Sees Nuclear Network Threat." *Washington Times*, 28 April 2004.

Levy, Jack S. "The Offensive/Defensive Balance of Military Technology: A Theoretical and Historical Analysis." *International Studies Quarterly* 28 (1984).

Lewis, Bernard. "License to Kill." *Foreign Affairs* 77, no. 6 (1998).

– "The Roots of Muslim Rage." *Atlantic Monthly*, September 1990.

Lichtblau, Eric. "Government Report on US Aviation Warns of Security Holes." *New York Times*, 14 March 2005.

Lindsey, George. "Canada, North American Security, and NORAD." CIIA Occasional Papers, *International Insights* 2, no. 3 (2004). Toronto: Canadian Institute of International Affairs, 2004.

– "Potential Contributions by the Canadian Armed Forces to the Defence of North America against Terrorism." *International Journal* 58, no. 3 (2003).

Ljunggren, David. "Ottawa Vows to Do More to Prevent Attacks on US." *Reuters*, 25 March 2004.

Loeb, Vernon. "Army Expansion Could Last 5 Years." *Washington Post*, 30 January 2004.

– "Chief Hopes to Quicken Army's Shift." *Washington Post*, 3 October 2003.

Lumpkin, John J. "US Says Al Qaeda Hurt But Not Broken." *Washington Times*, 24 April 2003.

– "US Says New Qaeda Figure Emerges." *Boston Globe*, 2 October 2003.

Lynn-Jones, Sean M. "Offense-Defense Theory and Its Critics." *Security Studies* 4, no. 4 (1995).

MacKenzie, Lewis. Testimony before the Standing Senate Committee on National Security and Defence, 3 May 2004.

Maher, Stephen. "Boost for Coast Guard Expected." *Halifax Herald*, 23 February 2005.

Manley, John P., Pedro Aspe, and William F. Weld. *Creating a North American Community.* New York: Council on Foreign Relations, Independent Task Force on the Future of North America, March 2005.

Martin, Paul. Address at CFB Gagetown. Gagetown, New Brunswick, 14 April 2004.

Mason, Dwight N. *Canadian Defense Priorities: What Might the United States Like to See?* Policy Papers on the Americas 15, study 1. Washington, DC: Center for Strategic and International Studies, 2004.

Matthews, William. "Momentum Builds for Single US Intel Chief." *Defense News*, 23 August 2004.

– "Triumph of Jointness." *Defense News*, 14 April 2003.

– "US Lawmakers Push 'Prompt Global Strike': Homeland UAVs, Special Forces Also Winners in 2004 Authorization Bill." *Defense News*, 24 November 2003.

– "US Watches for Cargo Use by Terrorists." *Defense News*, 24 March 2003.

McGrory, Daniel. "Two Years On, Bush May Be Losing War to Al Qaeda." *Times* (London), 10 September 2003.

McLaughlin, Abraham. "Why Sudan Has Become a Bush Priority." *Christian Science Monitor*, 30 June 2004.

Meisner, Tim. Testimony before the Standing Senate Committee on National Security and Defence, 17 February 2003.

"MI5 Chief: Defeating Islamic Terror Will Be a Long Haul." *Jerusalem Post*, 17 October 2003.

Minister's Monitoring Committee. *In the Service of the Nation: Canada's Citizen Soldiers for the 21st Century.* Ottawa: Department of National Defence, June 2000.

Mintz, John. "Bioterrorism Procedures Are Outlined: Bush Directive Specifies Agency Responsibilities." *Washington Post*, 29 April 2004.

– "Homeland Security Boosts Funds on Antimissile Plan." *Washington Post*, 19 September 2003.

– "US Officials Warn of New Tactics by Al Qaeda." *Washington Post*, 5 September 2003.

"More Troops to Afghanistan." *Toronto Star*, 14 February 2005.

Morton, Desmond. "'No More Disagreeable or Onerous Duty': Canadians and Military Aid of the Civil Power, Past, Present, Future." In *Canada's International Security Policy,* edited by David Dewitt and David Leyton-Brown. Scarborough, ON: Prentice Hall, 1995.

Murray, Douglas. "NORAD and US Nuclear Operations." In *Fifty Years of Canada-United States Security Cooperation,* edited by Joel J. Sokolsky and Joseph T. Jockel. Lewiston, NY: Edwin Meller Press, 1992.

Murray, Williamson, and Robert H. Scales Jr. *The Iraq War.* Cambridge: Harvard University Press, 2003.

National Commission on Terrorist Attacks upon the United States. *The 9/11 Commission Report.* Washington, DC: National Commission on Terrorist Attacks upon the United States, July 2004.

National Defense Panel. *Transforming Defense: National Security in the 21st Century.* Washington, DC: National Defense Panel, December 1997.

National Security Council. *National Security Strategy for a New Century.* Washington, DC: National Security Council, 1998.

– *National Security Strategy of the United States.* Washington, DC: National Security Council, 2002.

Naylor, Sean. "Overhauling the US Army." *Defense News*, 29 September 2003.

"The New Terrorism." *Economist*, 15 August 1998.

"The Next War, They Say." *Economist*, 6 August 1994.

Nickerson, Colin. "US-Canada Security Brings Frustration to Both Sides of Border." *Globe and Mail*, 20 January 2003.

"NORAD Could Evolve into North American NATO, Says US Military Leader." *Canadian Press*, 26 March 2004.

Office of Homeland Security. *National Strategy for Homeland Security*. Washington, DC: Office of Homeland Security, July 2002.

Office of Naval Research. *Naval Operations in an Ice-Free Arctic*. Arlington, VA: Office of Naval Research, 2001.

Parachini, John. "Putting WMD Terrorism into Perspective." *Washington Quarterly* 26, no. 4 (2003).

Paraskevas, Joe. "Make Coast Guard an Armed Military Force, Committee Urges." *Ottawa Citizen*, 1 April 2004.

Payne, Keith. *Deterrence in the Second Nuclear Age*. Lexington, KY: University Press of Kentucky, 1996.

– "NPR Moves US Beyond 'Balance of Terror.'" *Defense News*, 15 March 2004.

"Pentagon Realigns Military Structure." *Washington Times*, 18 April 2002.

Perry, William. "Preparing for the Next Attack." *Foreign Affairs* 80, no. 6 (2001).

Posen, Barry R. "The Struggle against Terrorism: Grand Strategy, Strategy, and Tactics." *International Security* 26, no. 3 (2001–02).

"Present at the Creation: America's World Role." *Economist*, 29 June 2002.

Prothero, P. Mitchell. "United States Ranked Fourth as Likely Terrorist Target." *Washington Times*, 19 August 2003.

"*Public Safety Act* Receives Royal Assent." Government of Canada news release, 6 May 2004.

Pugliese, David. "Anti-terror Radar Plan Tied Up in Red Tape." *Ottawa Citizen*, 11 April 2005.

– "Canada Aims to Prove Value of Micro-sats." *Defense News*, 1 September 2003.

– "Canada Revises Sensor Program." *Defense News*, 12 July 2004.

– "Canada Shifts Plan to Increase Special Forces." *Defense News*, 26 April 2004.

– "Canada to Develop Sensor to Track Satellites, Debris." *Defense News*, 28 January-3 February 2003.

– "Canada to Improve CF-18s' Targeting, Weapons." *Defense News*, 11 October 2004.

- "Canada to Try UAVs in Arctic." *Defense News*, 2 August 2004.
- "Canadian Navy Chief Inherits Small Purse." *Defense News*, 15 November 2004.
- "Canadian Project for Space-Based Sensor Moves to New Stage." *Defense News*, 19 July 2004.
- "Future Forces: Smart and Plugged In." *Ottawa Citizen*, 17 October 2004.
- "Navy Shops around for New Midsized Patrol Vessels." *Ottawa Citizen*, 12 July 2004.
- "Overhaul Will Boost Canada's Coastal Security." *Defense News*, 13 September 2004.
- "Part-Time Soldiers to Play Key Role in Civil Defence." *Ottawa Citizen*, 4 October 2004.
- "Space Program Could Feed Data to Missile Shield." *Ottawa Citizen*, 27 February 2005.
- "US Missile Plan Risks Arms Race, Canada Told." *Ottawa Citizen*, 17 July 2004.
- "US Wants Weapons in Space." *National Post*, 7 February 2004.

Purdy, Margaret. "Countering Terrorism: The Missing Pillar." *International Journal* 60, no. 1 (2004–05).

Quester, George. *Offense and Defense in the International System*. New York: Wiley, 1977.

Ratnam, Gopal. "Airborne Laser May Be Grounded." *Defense News*, 12 July 2004.

Record, Jeffrey. *Bounding the Global War on Terrorism*. Carlisle, PA: Strategic Studies Institute, US Army War College, 2003.

Reid, Tim. "Forty States 'Have Nuclear Capability.'" *Times Online*, 1 November 2003.

Rekai, Peter. *United States and Canadian Immigration Policies: Marching Together to Different Tunes*. Border Papers 171. Toronto: CD Howe Institute, 2002.

Risen, James. "Ex-government Officials Recommend Intelligence Overhaul." *New York Times*, 9 December, 2003.

Roach, Kent. *September 11: Consequences for Canada*. Montreal: McGill-Queen's University Press, 2003.

Roosevelt, Ann. "Strykers Turning In 'Extraordinary Performance.'" *Defense Daily*, 18 January 2005.

Rubin, Barry. "The Real Roots of Arab Anti-Americanism." *Foreign Affairs* 81, no. 6 (2002).

Rudner, Martin. "Contemporary Threats, Future Tasks: Canadian Intelligence and the Challenges of Global Security." In *Canada among Nations*

2002: A Fading Power, edited by Norman Hillmer and Maureen Appel Molot. Toronto: Oxford University Press, 2002.

"'Safe Third Country' Agreement to be Signed This Week." CBC *News Online*, 4 December 2002.

Sallot, Jeff. "Graham Defends Joining US Arms Interception Plan." *Globe and Mail*, 17 February 2004.

Scarborough, Rowan. "Special Ops Steal Show as Successes Mount in Iraq." *Washington Times*, 7 April 2003.

"Security and Prosperity Partnership of North America Established." Government of Canada news release, 23 March 2005.

Segal, Heather. "After So Much Spent on Security, Are We Secure Yet?" *Globe and Mail*, 31 March 2004.

Seper, Jerry. "FBI 'Reprioritized' after '01 Terror Attacks, Report Says." *Washington Times*, 5 October 2004.

– "Guarding America's Border." *Washington Times*, 8 December 2003.

Shenon, Philip. "US to Put Inspectors at Muslim Ports." *New York Times*, 12 June 2003.

Sherman, Jason. "Global Teams Angle for Slice of Warship." *Defense News*, 18–24 November 2002.

– "US Drafts Homeland Strategy." *Defense News*, 27 September 2004.

– "US Navy's Role Soars." *Defense News*, 3 March 2003.

– "US War on Terror Looms for QDR." *Defense News*, 25 October 2004.

Simon, Steven. "The New Terrorism: Securing the Nation against a Messianic Foe." *Brookings Review* 21, no.1 (2003).

Sirak, Michael. "America's BMD Stumbles." *Jane's Defence Weekly*, 1 May 2002.

Slobodian, Linda. "General Sees Reserve Force as Vital for Terror Response." *Calgary Herald*, 22 March 2004.

Sokolski, Henry. "Rethinking Bio-chemical Dangers." *Orbis* 44, no. 2 (2000).

Sokolsky, Joel. "The Bilateral Defence Relationship with the United States." In *Canada's International Security Policy*, edited by David Dewitt and David Leyton-Brown. Scarborough, ON: Prentice Hall, 1995.

Stairs, Denis. "9/11 Terrorism, Root Causes and All That: Policy Implications of the Socio-cultural Argument." *Policy Options* 23, no. 6 (2002).

Standing Committee on National Defence and Veterans Affairs. *Facing Our Responsibilities: The State of Readiness of the Canadian Forces*. Ottawa: Government of Canada, May 2002.

Standing Senate Committee on National Security and Defence. *Canadian Security and Military Preparedness*. Ottawa: Government of Canada, February 2002.

– *Defence of North America: A Canadian Responsibility.* Ottawa: Government of Canada, September 2002.

– *The Longest Under-Defended Borders in the World.* Ottawa: Government of Canada, October 2003.

– *The Myth of Security at Canada's Airports.* Ottawa: Government of Canada, January 2003.

Stern, Jessica. "The Protean Enemy." *Foreign Affairs* 82, no. 4 (2003).

Stern, Seth. "Military 'Transformation' Might Not Mean Smaller Forces." *Christian Science Monitor,* 7 May 2003.

"Survey of Islam and the West." *Economist,* 13 September 2003.

Svitak, Amy. "US Army, Navy Mull Lessons Learned in Afghanistan War." *Defense News,* 22–28 July 2002.

Taylor, Guy, and Tom Ramstack. "Ridge Adds 5,000 Air Marshals to Help Get 'Surge Capacity.'" *Washington Times,* 3 September 2003.

Tenet, George. "Worldwide Threat – Converging Dangers in a Post 9/11 World." Testimony before the Senate Armed Services Committee, 19 March 2002.

– "The Worldwide Threat in 2003: Evolving Dangers in a Complex World." Testimony before the Senate Select Committee on Intelligence, 11 February 2003.

– "The Worldwide Threat in 2004: Challenges in a Changing Global Context." Testimony before the Senate Armed Services Committee, 9 March 2004.

Thorne, Stephen. "NORAD Role Could Be Altered." *Canadian Press,* 24 February 2005.

Tibbetts, Janice. "Our Border 'Not a Conduit for Terrorists.'" *Ottawa Citizen,* 30 April 2003.

Tirpak, John A. "The Space Based Radar Plan." *Air Force Magazine* 85, no. 8 (2002).

"To Rescue Iraq, It's Time to Move On." *Economist,* 27 September 2003.

Tomlinson, Chris. "Military Stalks Terrorists in Africa." *Washington Times,* 1 January 2004.

"Transformed? A Survey of the Defence Industry." *Economist,* 20 July 2002.

Tyson, Ann Scott. "New US Strategy: 'Lily Pad' Bases." *Christian Science Monitor,* 10 August 2004.

Ullman, Richard H. "Redefining Security." *International Security* 8, no. 3 (1983).

"Update on Preparedness." *Washington Times,* 21 November 2003.

US Commission on National Security/21st Century. *New World Coming.* Washington, DC: US Commission on National Security/21st Century, 1999.

– *Road Map for National Security: Imperative for Change.* Washington, DC: US Commission on National Security/21st Century, 2001.

– *Seeking a National Strategy.* Washington, DC: US Commission on National Security/21st Century, 2000.

US Commission on Weak States and National Security. *On the Brink: Weak States and US National Security.* Washington, DC: Center for Global Development, 8 June 2004.

US Department of State. *Patterns of Global Terrorism 2002.* Washington, DC: US Department of State, 30 April 2003.

– *Patterns of Global Terrorism 2003.* Washington, DC: US Department of State, 29 April 2004.

"US Launches Aerial Surveillance of Border." *Globe and Mail,* 20 August 2004.

Van Evera, Stephen. *Causes of War: Power and the Roots of Conflict.* Ithaca: Cornell University Press, 1999.

– "Offense, Defense and the Causes of War." *International Security* 22, no. 4 (1998).

VanderKlippe, Nathan. "Arctic a Potential Terror Target." *Edmonton Journal,* 19 September 2004.

Vice Chief of the Defence Staff. *Rethinking the Total Force: Aligning the Defence Team for the 21st Century.* Ottawa: Department of National Defence, November 1999.

Vickers, Melana Zyla. "LCS Could Bolster Defense against Terror." *Defense News,* 14 July 2003.

Walt, Stephen. "Beyond Bin Laden." *International Security* 26, no. 3 (2001–02).

Ward, John. "Henault Hopes Defence Review Will Reveal What Government Expects, Will Pay." *Canadian Press,* 10 July 2002.

"Warding off Missiles: An American Dream." *Economist,* 6 December 2003.

"Warning about WMD." *Washington Times,* 25 June 2004.

Wattie, Chris. "Forces to 'Flex Muscles' in North." *National Post,* 27 March 2004.

– "Radar Stations to Guard Canada by Sea." *National Post,* 4 December 2003.

– "Reservists Touted as Terrorism Fighters." *National Post,* 8 January 2004.

"Where Paul Martin Should Lead Canada." *Globe and Mail*, 15 December 2003.

Williams, Rick. Testimony before the Standing Senate Committee on National Security and Defence, 17 March 2003.

"Worldwide Web of Nuclear Danger." *Economist*, 28 February 2004.

Wright, Robert. Testimony before the Standing Senate Committee on National Security and Defence, 23 February 2004.

Wright, Quincy. *A Study of War*. Vol. 1. Chicago: University of Chicago Press, 1942.

Index